Basic Communities

Basic Communities

A Practical Guide
for Renewing Neighborhood Churches

Thomas Maney, MM

WINSTON PRESS

Scripture texts used in this work are taken from the *New American Bible,* copyright © 1970 by the Confraternity of Christian Doctrine, Washington, D.C. Used by permission of the copyright owner. All rights reserved.

Cover design: Terry Dugan

Nihil Obstat: James Chisholm
             Censor Librorum
             April .4, 1983
Imprimatur: + Paul F. Anderson
             Bishop of Duluth
             April 5, 1983

Library of Congress Catalog Card Number: 84-51039

ISBN: 0-86683-857-0

Printed in the United States of America

5   4   3   2   1

Winston Press, Inc.
430 Oak Grove
Minneapolis, Minnesota 55403

*This book is dedicated to Kathy Cordova,
my initial and invaluable editor,
and to her husband, José,
source of encouragement and support*

ACKNOWLEDGMENTS

I wish to thank the Maryknoll Fathers and our Superior General, the Reverend James P. Noonan, MM, for permission to dedicate myself completely to evangelization through the Parish Neighborhood Renewal Ministry.

I also wish to thank Bishop Paul F. Anderson for his invaluable encouragement, counsel, and support.

Special thanks go to those who read, corrected, and offered suggestions on the manuscript: my Parish Neighborhood Renewal Evangelization Community (the Reverend James Scheuer, the Reverend Patrick Carey, Sister Mary Joan Gerads, OSF, Sister Patricia Schneider, SSND, Mrs. Anna Chernugal, and Eugene A. Skelton); the Reverend Robert Voigt; Bob and Kathy Pauly; John and Sarah Maney; Bud and Mary Schlick; Jane Eschweiler; Monsignor Terrance W. Berntson; Sister Paula Pohlman, OSF; the Reverend John K. Halbert, MM; the Reverend Fidelis C. Goodman, MM; and the Dominican preaching team, especially the Reverend Ralph Rogawski, OP, and Sister Helen Raycraft, OP.

Much encouragement was offered by the Sisters of St. Francis House, Duluth: Sisters Adella Blonigen, OSF, Lorraine Olmscheid, OSF, and Rosaria Hagel, OSF. The following contributed much to the realization of this work: James and Marilyn Manderfeld, Catherine Connaker, Helen Allison, Sister Mary Charles McGough, OSB, Mary Sue House, Lorraine Skelton, Lawrence Chernugal, and those of the Maryknoll Development House in Minneapolis.

In a special way I wish to thank Sister Mary Richard Boo, OSB, who helped me in stylistic matters, and Sister Margaret James Laughlin, OSB, typist of the final manuscript.

CONTENTS

Foreword by Bishop Paul F. Anderson . . . ix

Preface . . . xi

The Search
1. My Search for Faith-Community Formation . . . 2

The Goal
2. The Christian Goal: To Evangelize . . . 12

The Basis
3. Prayer Paves the Way for Parish Neighborhood Renewal . . . 20
4. Beginning Evangelization: The Laity's Initial Role . . . 26

The Process
5. The Home-Visiting Ministry . . . 34
6. Experiencing the Neighborhood Mission . . . 41
7. Renewal Touches Parishioners and Pastor Alike . . . 48
8. Developing Ministries for Service . . . 54

The Results
9. Renewed Neighborhoods, Vehicles of Social Change . . . 62
10. Joyful Christians Bring New Life to the Parish . . . 69

The Future
11. The Core Team's Ongoing Contact with the Parish . . . 76

A Blessing for My Readers . . . 83

Appendix A: The Spirit of the Evangelization Community . . . 84

Appendix B: Mission of Renewal in the Holy Spirit to Initiate Basic Church Communities . . . 92

Appendix C: Flow Chart and Checklist for Flow Chart . . . 98

FOREWORD

I live in a neighborhood that could be defined as upper middle-class. Many of the houses are architectural gems designed in the early part of the century. They are surrounded by nice lawns and beautiful shrubbery that are pleasing to the eye and to the wide-angle lens of a photographic hobbyist. My neighborhood could be defined as the quiet, reserved side of town.

But there are other sections that could also be called middle-class, or even poverty areas, where the dwellings are huddled close together, with a twenty-five-foot frontage that gives one the impression of getting the maximum amount of dwelling on the minimum amount of land. Whether one wants to class these areas as high-rent or low-rent does not really matter when the sociologist begins to assess the quality of life found there. The spirit of darkness that overshadows the contemporary person makes no great distinction between classes and bank accounts. The loneliness that besets the elderly person living in one room, and surviving on Social Security, is the same loneliness that eats into the heart of a wealthy person living in the suburbs. The fear that one's children may give way to the pressures of drug addiction, violence, or alcoholism is a universal one that passes beyond social status or the quality of housing.

How fortunate for us that the Second Vatican Council focused its attention on the renewal of the Church, not so much in its institutional forms as in its understanding of itself as the People of God! Although there have been dramatic changes in ritual, sacrament, word, and structure, the greatest work of renewal has to do with the human heart. It is a renewal of minds and lives, a new attitude based on our relationship to Jesus and to one another. It is the building of the Kingdom that is within.

More than twenty years have passed since Vatican II began its world-shaking sessions. But it is only now that one begins to see the real work of the council changing the lives of people. A new way of looking at Church is gradually surfacing in the daily life and activities of God's people. Because of programs like Marriage Encounter, Cursillo, TEC, and Spiritual Retreats, there is a growing consciousness that the living Body of Christ, empowered by the Holy Spirit, is made of flesh and blood.

Five years ago when Sister Joan Gerads and Father Thomas Maney told me that the Church would be renewed in the neighborhoods of the parish, I was skeptical. Now I have the evidence of their work here in the local Church. I have seen with my eyes and heard with my ears the wonderful things that have transpired in all kinds of neighborhoods, poor as well as upper- and middle-class. People who a few months ago were living in areas marked by alienation, loneliness, and fear are now coming together in small groups on a weekly basis to pray and discuss what it means to be Church. Many have told me personally that this has been the greatest single thing that has ever happened to them in recent years.

This little book, *Basic Communities: A Practical Guide for Renewing Neighborhood Churches,* is the story of this experience. It is told simply in language that is easily understood. It gives the step-by-step explanation of how neighborhood parish community can be built, and is being built, in the heartland of America.

It is my prayer that it will have a wide circulation and that those who long for renewal in our times will find here a method and approach that is both effective and lasting.

Paul F. Anderson
Bishop of Duluth, Minnesota

PREFACE

Overview of Parish Neighborhood Renewal

"Here I stand, knocking at the door. If anyone hears me calling and opens the door, I will enter his house and have supper with him, and he with me."

—Revelation 3:20

Today there is a new awareness that Jesus is renewing our neighborhoods. The results are exciting, unexpected, resurrectional. The New Pentecost envisioned by Pope John XXIII is here! Our Lord is calling all Catholics to participate in the fullness of their vocation as members of church communities.

Vatican II recognized our need to read the signs of the times, and our times clearly cry out for a deepening sense of practical Christian living in contrast to lonely, noninvolved lifestyles. Mother Teresa spoke of this need when she pointed out the "spiritual hunger" prevalent in the United States. In response to this interior deprivation, the Holy Spirit seems to be calling Christians to a communal way of life centered on Jesus.

The practice of Christian community life is as new as the post-Vatican II era of communal Catholicism and as old as the apostolic Church. Scripture explicitly states that the basic church community is the core of Christian living. The first Christians "devoted themselves to the apostles' instruction and the communal life, to the breaking of bread and the prayers" (Acts 2:42).

Basic Communities: A Practical Guide for Renewing Neighborhood Churches presents an exciting breakthrough for church renewal. The Basic Church Community—or as we call it, the Neighborhood Church Community—is an instrument that can create a whole new intimacy of Christian sharing and renewal within the Church. All the goals of the Call to Action of 1978 of the United States bishops are met by the Neighborhood Church Community.

I present in story form and with experiential vividness the way in which the Parish Neighborhood Renewal Ministry, of which I am a founding member, has actually formed over 300 Neighborhood Church Communities in middle-class American parishes. These parishes are of varying sizes and locations. They range from large city parishes of 2,500 families in Minneapolis and Duluth, Minnesota, and in Lubbock, Texas, through small cities and towns to rural parishes of 75 or 100 families. Each parish, regardless of its size or lifestyle, has felt the surge of spiritual renewal.

This book tells in detail how your parish can form these communities. It relates the remarkable changes that individuals and parishes have experienced. It describes the Latin American experience that brought about the introduction of a new way to form Neighborhood Church Communities and the manner in which the Latin American experience was adapted to the North American personality. Home Visitation was the breakthrough that made this adaptation possible.

The approach of the Parish Neighborhood Renewal Ministry to renewal is to form Neighborhood Church Communities in the familiar neighborhood setting. The seed of a church community germinates in a five-day mission during which neighbors share their faith experiences with one another. This is possible because when a host family offers its home for the five evenings, a sense of neighborhood starts immediately.

A sense of intimacy in neighborhoods is difficult to achieve in the contemporary North American lifestyle. Our affluence has become a barrier to neighborhood relationships. The American automobile has shattered neighborhood interdependency. We are free to seek goods, services, and social life away from the neighborhood. Even our church community is often miles away from where we live.

Recently at one of the neighborhood missions, neighbors who had lived a little over one block apart for twenty-three years became acquainted for the first time. It becomes clear that for Americans, living in a neighborhood doesn't automatically mean knowing those who live around them. It is becoming even rarer that personal friendships are formed between next-door neighbors.

The Parish Neighborhood Renewal Ministry, then, is a response to Vatican II in which lay persons, united with their priests, can renew the Church in the Spirit. These Neighborhood Church Communities involve all people, cut across age groups, and include different theological tendencies, from the more traditional to the innovative. The Neighborhood Church Community doesn't compete with existing church-sponsored groups; rather, it draws out the gifts of each individual and of every group to serve the Neighborhood Church. It aims to give service to all in the neighborhood, non-Christian as well as Christian.

In the Parish Neighborhood Renewal Minisry, personal conversion is experienced through an evangelization mission. All people need continual conversion experiences. This includes *me,* whether I am a pastor, a member of the parish team, or any concerned lay person. St. Paul teaches us that such "spiritual recycling" is necessary:

> You must lay aside your former way of life and the old self which deteriorates through illusion and desire, and acquire a fresh, spiritual way of thinking. You must put on that new man created in God's image, whose justice and holiness are born of truth . . . the truth that is in Jesus.
>
> —Ephesians 4:22-24, 21

Through the neighborhood mission, God's grace touches many hearts and God's blessings are called down on all the neighbors. Converted people experience a new power born of God's more intimate presence in their lives. The amazing fact is that when converted people come together in church community, there is a greater force present than the sum of the power of each individual. "Where two or three are gathered in my [Jesus'] name, there am I in their midst" (Matthew 18:20). That is why in the Parish Neighborhood Renewal Ministry we say, "1 + 1 = 3."

The goal of the Parish Neighborhood Renewal Ministry is to implant a Christian seed in a neighborhood—a seed that will foster relationships of love, trust, and concern. Jesus is recognized as living in the neighborhood setting, especially within the lives of converted Christians. The converted Christian receives a new vision of social justice and a desire to change the social structures that impede wholesome growth and freedom.

As Neighborhood Church Communities grow and flourish, the effects of renewal become evident in a parish setting. A revitalized attitude toward prayer, liturgy, and scripture reading emerges. The renewed laity perform as dynamic apostles of the Good News. Neighborhood Church Communities become an added source of leadership in the parish. Pastors and parish staffs are delighted because they find converted parishioners eager to cooperate and support their ministry.

In the following chapters I share practical information and personal experiences as well as the sociological and psychological basis for faith-community development. To help you get started, I have included three appendices that contain the outlines of the actual mission and other useful information. Many people have encouraged the Parish Neighborhood Renewal Ministry Core Team to share what we have learned in our ministry. It is in this spirit of sharing that I have written *Basic Communities: A Practical Guide for Renewing Neighborhood Churches.*

Father Tom Maney, MM
Parish Neighborhood Renewal Ministry
1950 E. 25th St.
Hibbing, Minnesota 55746
Phone: (218) 262-2482

THE SEARCH

CHAPTER ONE

My Search for Faith-Community Formation

The Basic Church Community, as a *community,* consists of entire families, adults and youth, brought together intimately in faith through interpersonal relationships. Being *Church,* it is a community of faith, hope and love. It celebrates the Word of God by living it. . . . It fulfills the mission of the Church and is united to church authority by approved coordinators. It is called *basic* since it has a small number of committed members who form a cell as a part of a larger community. When it is truly worthy of the title "Church," the Basic Church Community is able to promote its own spiritual growth.

> —*Puebla Document,* Third Latin
> American Bishops Conference,
> #641 (author's translation)

It's apparent today that God the Father is sending the Holy Spirit to renew the Church. Certainly one of the most exciting signs of this renewal is the proliferation of Basic Church Communities throughout the world, especially since Pope Paul VI recognized their value in 1975 in his Apostolic Exhortation *On Evangelization in the Modern World.* Four years later, *Time* (May 7, 1979) said there were some 150,000 Basic Communities in Latin America alone. The *St. Anthony Messenger* of September 1979 calculated that there were about 4,000 Basic Church Communities functioning in the United States at that same time. (The great majority of these were among Spanish-speaking Americans.) More recently, the Parish Neighborhood Renewal Ministry, of which I am a member, has been responsible for forming over 300 Basic Church Communities in Midwestern parishes alone from 1978 to 1983.

Even earlier, however, the Basic Church Community had received its first general acceptance in Latin America in 1968 at the Second General Assembly of Bishops at Medellín, Columbia. Again at Puebla, Mexico, in 1979, in their Third General Assembly, these same bishops reemphasized the formation of Basic Church Communities as a top priority for the Latin American Church. In 1978, during their episcopal conferences, the bishops of Asia and Africa chose the formation of Basic Church Communities as their number one goal. It seems evident, too, that the goals of the bishops of the United States stated in their Call to Action of 1978 can be fulfilled by the Basic Church Community. We might well ask, then, what specific and long-felt needs the Basic Church Communities can meet.

Levels of Church Community

An initial reminder: Although there is but one Body of Christ, there are different structural levels of his Church. The smallest Church, of course, is the family. Built upon that are the basic church community (also called the neighborhood Church), to be discussed throughout this book; the parish Church; the diocesan Church; and finally the universal Church. Each level builds on the other, and each Church must be well and strong if the Body of Christ is to flourish.

One reason we need Basic Church Communities, then, is that God showers these "levels" of persons with a variety of gifts. We need to go to one another to give and to receive in community what can never be achieved by any individual alone. God distributes his gifts to individuals for the good of the group. In the same manner, he gives each small group a special charism or gift for the good of the parish; each parish, for the upbuilding of the diocese; and each diocese, for the strengthening of the universal Church.

These Basic Church Communities, when fully developed, become an answer, too, to the shortage of clergy because they can promote their own spiritual growth. It was the vision of the Latin American Church—heavily populated, yet lacking in numbers of clergy—in its search for a means to shepherd its people that now helps us in North America to rediscover the neighborhood Church.

Besides the gifts that God showers on the different levels of · Church, gifts are given to each nation for the community of nations. Venezuela's gift to the world, for example, is its generous love. Venezuelans by their nature have a warm, gregarious, trusting attitude toward other people that endears them to more sophisticated nations. They know how to celebrate life. Persons are more important that material goods. I found the Venezuelan spirit of community and wholehearted sharing an inspiration for the entire Parish Neighborhood Renewal Ministry. In North America, sadly enough, we have seen a breakdown of this neighborhood friendliness and sharing; we might well look to our Venezuelan counterparts in parish renewal for a model here.

In brief, then: Through the Neighborhood Church, the Body of Christ can flourish on a parish level. This is the compelling reason for the Parish Neighborhood Renewal Ministry.

My Latin American Experience

I became involved in the formation of communities from the very beginning of my missionary years in Chile. In 1956 I was assigned to the diocese of Talca, whose bishop was Manuel Larrain. Bishop Larrain was the great South American leader for social change, and as the first president of CELAM, the Latin American Bishops Conference, he exerted great influence. He brought the Basic Church Communities into reality in his diocese of Talca and was responsible for initiating them in many parts of Chile as well as in other Latin American countries. I spent ten years working with him on pastoral planning as a pastor, rural dean, and diocesan consultor until his death in an automobile accident in 1966.

During my first years in Chile, I brought my rural people together to solve their felt needs. We fixed up roads and schools, obtained a water-supply system for a small community, planted thousands of trees on the barren coastal slopes, cleaned up trash, and constructed community centers. As we worked, I wanted my people to come together in faith communities and form Neighborhood Church. But this did not happen. I had even hoped that, as a result of all these community action projects, the people would continue helping one another and would reach out to neighboring areas. Rarely did this occur. Rather, these groups disbanded as quickly as a given project was completed. But it was my first step in discovering the process of church community formation.

The second phase of my education was from 1962 to 1964, when Bishop Larrain launched a total diocesan effort to form Basic Church Communities. I entered the work with enthusiasm. Teams of priests, sisters, and laypersons were formed. We spent two weeks at a time in a *barrio*—a neighborhood of a city—or in a country sector to bring the people together for church renewal.

When the renewal program arrived in my rural deanery, I was mission coordinator for eight parishes. We formed twenty-nine Basic Church Communities. These communities were successful—enduring over time because of their religious basis. Five years later, twenty-five of the twenty-nine communities were still functioning, although with different degrees of intensity. Still, something was missing; the spark to energize Catholics to be fully committed to serve Jesus and their neighbors was simply not there.

In January of 1975, in God's providence, I met three people who were to change my life and who would give me the answer for forming true neighborhood church community. They showed me the key ingredient for developing the neighborhood Church.

I was a delegate from Chile to the Latin American Charismatic Conference at Aguas Buenas, Puerto Rico. On my way I stopped over at Caracas, Venezuela, where I met Sister Mary Joan Gerads, OSF, a delegate from Venezuela. During the conference we became friends, and she told me about two Dominican religious who were on the program at the conference: Father Ralph Rogawski, OP, and Sister Helen Raycraft, OP. These two missionaries spoke on their experience in forming neighborhood church communities by leading individuals through a personal conversion experience. As soon as they mentioned the conversion experience, I recognized the element that had eluded me in my experiences with Chilean community formation.

The method of forming Neighborhood Church Communities out of a conversion experience had its beginning with Father Ralph, who had had the courage to say, "I'm quitting this organizational rat race. I'm going to ask God to show me a new way to do his will."

Father Ralph, a Midwesterner, was already an experienced missionary when he was assigned to the Santa Cruz, Bolivia, area in 1967. He had had extensive experience in forming social action groups, labor unions, and community self-help organizations. Sister Helen Raycraft was working in a nearby barrio, a poor, densely populated area. Sharing mutual interests and work efforts, they soon formed a Dominican missionary team for community organization in the barrios.

Over the next several years they developed a leadership training program and presented it in twenty barrios and small towns in and about Santa Cruz, Bolivia. Soon it became clear to them that leadership training alone would not solve three general weaknesses of their leaders: a lack of motivation, insufficient unity, and an overdependence on the missionary team to inspire them. Both Sister Helen and Father Ralph were attending multiple meetings, were always on the go, and were becoming increasingly frustrated at the poor carry-over from their efforts.

At that time, Father Ralph still had no major doubts about the ultimate value of their efforts to help people to organize themselves, yet he felt a need to take time to reflect on the effectiveness of what he and Sister Helen were doing. Accordingly, he took what he jokingly calls his month of "retirement." No sooner had he begun this month of release-time than he came to a sudden decision: He simply and emphatically declared to himself, "I quit! I've had it! There has to be a better way to help our people."

So he began to pray. A week passed, and nothing happened. Since he had retired from all organizational activity, his fellow priests began to ask if he was physically sick. After three weeks they asked, "Is he mentally ill?" Father Ralph continued to pray. A month passed with no apparent answer to his prayer. He himself began to question if God was going to answer him, but he kept on. It was only after the fifth week that a new approach became clear to him. He had spent his "retirement" in rediscovering the effectiveness of prayer, in reading and meditating on the Scriptures, and in rethinking the needs of his people.

Father Ralph was determined to change the thrust of his apostolate from community development projects to faith-oriented communities. Simultaneously Sister Helen arrived at the same conclusion. After sharing their personal experiences, they decided to try the religious approach with the people in a destitute barrio of some five thousand people. In Barrio Fillin, two miles outside Santa Cruz, they called the people together to talk about Jesus, to pray, and to sing a bit. The attendance far surpassed the usual turnout for a community action meeting. After this first night's gathering, the people asked that the meeting be extended to five consecutive evenings.

What was exciting for Father Ralph and Sister Helen was that they saw enthusiasm and deep attitudinal changes in the people; in other words, they were witnessing fundamental conversion experiences. Unity and a renewal of faith developed among the people as the power of the Spirit took hold of those Bolivians. The people wanted to continue meeting on their own and Father Ralph and Sister Helen recognized that the people no longer needed to depend on them for motivation. Parish Neighborhood Renewal Ministry had been born in that barrio! Shortly afterward, Father Ralph and Sister Helen led the five-night mission in a second barrio; again the mission brought excellent turnouts and dramatic, permanent changes in people's lives.

During the early 1970s, Father Ralph and Sister Helen continued to form Basic Church Communities in Bolivia. First they tackled the challenges of renewal in a huge parish in Santa Cruz with an estimated population of thirty thousand. After assisting the La Crosse, Wisconsin, priests in charge of that parish, their team moved on to start renewal in other parishes. As a Dominican team, they were then invited to work in Colombia and in 1974 were invited to San Bartolomé parish, Maracay, Venezuela. This parish was staffed by the St. Cloud, Minnesota, diocesan priests and the Franciscan Sisters of Little Falls, Minnesota.

Father James Minette, pastor of San Bartolomé parish, had founded the parish ten years before the Dominican team arrived. He said that for those ten years his pastoral work had been like trying to push a heavy rock up a mountain. After Father Ralph and Sister Helen arrived and formed the Neighborhood Church Communities, he saw a dramatic change in the parishioners. With the help of the new leadership and the change in spirit in the neighborhoods, he found that the rock seemed to roll by itself. As he said, "Sometimes I had to run to catch up to my people."

Sister Joan Gerads was one of the Franciscan Sisters working with Father Minette when Father Ralph and Sister Helen came to Maracay. Sister Joan had arrived in Venezuela in 1970 with a Ph.D. in sociology, with the twin specialties of medical sociology and community development. She came with the sociological tools for community formation.

In the years before the arrival of the Dominican team, she too had experienced the need to form Neighborhood Church Communities and was searching for the means to accomplish this. As a sociologist, she saw clearly that having people come together in temporary socioeconomic groups to fulfill a need was not the same as establishing Basic Church Communities. She recognized that the method of Father Ralph and Sister Helen was the answer to her search for how to form those communities.

Our meeting in Puerto Rico and my subsequent visit to Maracay, Venezuela, convinced me that I too had found the answer. We began to explore and discern in prayer the idea of forming a team similar to that of our Dominican colleagues.

In 1975 Sister Joan and I worked together at various times in Venezuela. At the beginning of 1976, the Maryknoll Chile Region invited Sister Joan for a two-month stay in Chile to share her experience with Basic Church Communities. We worked as a team forming such communities in Talca and Temuco. Later I was transferred to Venezuela, but after only two months there I suffered a heart attack. In August of 1976 I returned to the United States and had open-heart surgery in Minneapolis.

At the end of 1977, after Sister Joan had returned to the United States, we met again and began to envision forming an evangelization community to work full time at renewing parishes. Bishop Paul Anderson of Duluth encouraged us to establish the Parish Neighborhood Renewal Ministry. He suggested that we spend a week in prayer and reflection as preparation for composing our lifestyle agreement. He then assigned one of the priests of the diocese to accompany us in our beginning missionary efforts. Since that time, our Neighborhood Renewal Evangelization Community has grown to seven persons—two sisters, two laypersons, and three priests.

The crucial development for our North American experience of the Neighborhood Church Community was Sister Joan's discovery of how to bring Catholic neighbors together. Our first two attempts in the United States had had limited success. We had given a general invitation to the families of the neighborhood and had asked the host family to invite their neighbors. But we discovered that Catholic neighbors often do not know one another. We found that neighbors were reluctant to believe they were truly welcomed in one another's homes. North Americans seemed to need several personal invitations before they would respond.

While reading Chapter 10 of the Gospel of Luke, Sister Joan came upon the technique for bringing Catholic neighbors together. Jesus sent seventy-two disciples out two by two to proclaim his coming: He "sent them in pairs before him to every town and place he intended to visit." Here again was the age-old solution to the closed-in neighborhoods of North America. Going

forth two by two to bless the Catholic families of the neighborhood and invite them to the five-day mission indeed proved to
be the answer.

The Parish Neigbhorhood Renewal Ministry grew out of our
Latin American experiences, but we had discovered how to adapt
it to meet the spiritual and social needs of North American
parishes. What surprised us was the eager response of people
hungry for sharing their faith in their daily lives with the persons
close to them. During our five years with the Parish Neighborhood Renewal Ministry in the United States, we have developed an avenue for parish renewal. We offer you our findings as a
guide for bringing laity and pastors to new beginnings.

THE GOAL

CHAPTER TWO

The Christian Goal: To Evangelize

Since the whole Church is missionary, and the work of evangelization is a basic duty of the People of God, this sacred Synod summons all to a deep interior renewal. Thus, from a vivid awareness of their own responsibility for spreading the gospel, they will do their share in missionary work among the nations.

> —*Documents of Vatican II,*
> "The Missionary Activity of
> the Church," paragraph 35

To sense what is happening to individuals and neighborhoods through the Parish Neighorhood Renewal program, the reader needs to understand the essence of evangelization. Evangelization has an *inward* and an *outward* effect. It is the complete penetration of Jesus into every cell and molecule of a human being. Jesus forms or reforms a person's judgment, value system, interests, thoughts, inspirations, and way of life. In other words, we have what St. Paul calls "the new man," or a converted person. (In contrast, the nonconverted person is likely to remain in self-contemplation and passiveness in relationship with the Lord and others.)

Vatican II has renewed the Church's understanding of the laity's right and duty to participate actively in evangelizing the world:

The laity derive the right and duty with respect to the
apostolate from their union with Christ their Head. . . .
They are assigned to the apostolate by the Lord himself. . . . Indeed, the law of love, which is the Lord's
greatest commandment, impels all the faithful to promote
God's glory through the spread of His kingdom. . . . On all
Christians therefore is laid the splendid burden of working
to make the divine message of salvation known and accepted by all . . . throughout the world.

> —*Documents of Vatican II,*
> "Decree on the Apostolate
> of the Laity," paragraph 3

As members of the living Christ, *all* the Faithful have been
incorporated into Him and made like unto Him. . . . Hence
all are duty-bound to cooperate in the expansion and growth
of His Body. . . . Therefore, *all* sons [and daughters] of the
Church should have a lively awareness of their responsibility
to the world. . . . They should spend their energies in the
work of evangelization.

> —*Documents of Vatican II,*
> "Decree on the Missionary Activity
> of the Church," paragraph 36
> (emphasis added)

Clearly the Church's documents are saying that it is the duty
and right of the laity to evangelize.

One powerful effect of evangelization is the upsetting of all the
worldly values that permeate humankind. Because evangelization has one end—to bring the whole world to Jesus Christ—it is
absolutely opposed to those standards that Pope Paul VI
described as being "in contrast with the Word of God and the plan
of salvation" (*On Evangelization in the Modern World,* paragraph
19).

Because of this necessarily disruptive effect of evangelization,
the missionary activity of the Church has recently been under
attack for "imposing" beliefs on others and restricting their liberty. Pope Paul VI answers this attack:

It would certainly be an error to impose something on the consciences of our brethren. But to propose to their consciences the truth of the Gospel and salvation in Jesus Christ, with complete clarity and with a total respect for the free options which it presents, . . . far from being an attack on religious liberty, is fully to respect that liberty, which offers the choice of a way that even nonbelievers consider noble and uplifting. . . . It would be useful if every Christian and every evangelizer were to pray about the following thought: Men can gain salvation also in other ways, by God's mercy, even though we do not preach the Gospel to them; but as for us, can we gain salvation if through negligence or fear or shame . . . or as a result of false ideas, we fail to preach it? For that would be to betray the call of God, who wishes the seed to bear fruit through the voice of the ministers of the Gospel; and it will depend on us whether this grows into trees and produces its full fruit.

—*On Evangelization in the Modern World,* paragraph 80

The Evangelical Role of the Parish

I have spoken of the need to form Neighborhood Church Communities through a basic evangelization mission. Jesus gives the grace of conversion, but he uses people as his agents. Because Jesus' work is accomplished through the mission of the Neighborhood Church Community, the team that gives the five-day mission must itself be a sign of God's power and love and at the same time have the talents and the expertise to transmit God's presence to the people of the neighborhood. It is the goal of the Renewal Core Team not only to be such a team but also to leave another such team formed in the parish after the first six-week period.

As lay people are touched at the neighborhood mission, the Renewal Core Team through prayer and discernment begins incorporating into the mission team those persons who appear to have the gifts of teaching and witnessing. People who formerly were reserved, indifferent, or timid often change by the grace of the Holy Spirit. People bloom as they offer their hidden talents to the Lord. As the Renewal Core Team works with those new parish team members, we recognize their strong qualities and blend the persons into a team. The pastor is closely included so that when the Core Team leaves, he may assume his role of affirming and encouraging this team of lay evangelizers. Once the Renewal Core Team has departed, the parish mission team, supported by the pastor and parish staff, will take on the primary responsibility of incorporating the rest of the parish into Neighborhood Church Communities.

During the six-week renewal period, some five or six Neighborhood Church Communities are usually formed in a parish. This means that between 200 and 240 parish families have been visited. Most parish teams find that one neighborhood mission each month is all they can handle. Lay people are volunteers. They usually have limited time to offer to the program. Still, if one neighborhood mission is scheduled each month, in one year up to 600 families can be visited. This means that as many as sixteen Neighborhood Renewal Groups will continue sharing Christian life together.

Our Renewal Core Team has observed some marvelous successes in parish renewal. For example, in one parish, the parish team completed the mission in the outlying geographical areas not touched by the Renewal Core Team. Now ten groups are actively sharing life in that parish of 480 families.

Evangelization on the Diocesan Level

Renewal work is church work. This presupposes that our renewal work proceeds with the permission of competent authority. Moreover, we envision a diocesan team united with its bishop to form an evangelization community. This concept has had its beginnings in the two dioceses where the Parish Neighborhood Renewal Ministry has been active from one to three years. In the

Duluth and St. Cloud dioceses we have "extended teams" or
diocesan mission teams that are responsible for the whole
diocese. The Renewal Core Team counts on the prayer support
of the extended team as well as the latter's active cooperation in
the mission work. Also, the members of the extended team give
presentations of the Parish Neighborhood Renewal Ministry to
additional parishes, help with the Renewal Core Team's newslet-
ter, counsel others, and participate in healing prayer.

For our part, the Renewal Core Team maintains contact with
these diocesan teams, offers them spiritual direction for their
personal growth, and invites them to participate in the retreats
and workshops we sponsor.

Some Individual Voices

When Jesus was beginning his "mission team," he went about
inviting people to follow him. "As he made his way along the Sea of
Galilee, he observed Simon and his brother Andrew casting their
nets into the sea; they were fishermen. Jesus said to them,
'Come after me; I will make you fishers of men.' They immediately abandoned their nets and became his followers" (Mark
1:16-18). Jesus' invitation is a deep personal experience that gives
a sense of freedom to accept it or not. Just as he did two thousand
years ago, today Jesus is still inviting "fishers of men." But each
one who accepts the invitation does so for different reasons.

Mrs. Lois Paull is one of the Parish Neighborhood Renewal
Ministry's extended team members. Lois relates:

Neighborhood Renewal came to St. Leo's parish at a time
when I was searching and asking God for direction and
guidance in my life. I had recently lost my husband and son.
Now I wondered where and how God wanted to use me. At
the first meeting with Father Tom and Sister Joan, I decided
working in the renewal was something I could and should
get involved in. I became a member of the parish mission
team, helped with home visiting and the missions in the
homes. This was a great experience and very rewarding.

My family and I received many blessings while I worked and prayed with these beautiful Christian friends. It was a time of real spiritual growth for me. I have never known such peace, joy, and love. Thank God for the Parish Neighborhood Renewal Ministry and the way it blessed my life.

Mrs. Paull was open and looking for involvement; the Lord had only to offer and she accepted his call. With Clarence Zylla of St. Mary's Cathedral parish, it was a different situation. When Clarence was asked to offer his home as the first host home in the parish, he thought there was to be a one-evening meeting. This much he accepted. Only after the Core Team had visited his home did he realize that it was a longer commitment. Now he quips, "God tricked me!" Nonetheless, he says:

It has been an exciting experience. At the close of the mission, I was chosen to be one of the group's servant-leaders. My wife and I joined the mission team and helped begin other groups. At the same time we assisted at our group's weekly meeting. My wife and I have always gotten more from these meetings than we contributed. We have developed into a concerned and caring unit, and the Lord has bestowed innumerable blessings on us. I am now more conscious of the fact that Jesus lives and answers prayers.

For Gene Skelton, the Neighborhood Renewal experience was God's invitation to full-time involvement in the ministry on the diocesan level. Gene is a Parish Neighborhood Renewal diocesan coordinator and a member of our Core Team Evangelization Community. He is married, is in his fifties, and has had extensive teaching and community development experience. He and his wife Lorraine spent ten years in Central America, first with the Peace Corps and later in community development work. But Gene states, "I never found peace in my life, nor could I settle down. I was forever searching and feeling unfulfilled."

He explains:

We returned to the United States from Central America in 1975. I began to have a strong desire to be with prayerful people. I found these people in a prayer group in my own parish. They taught me how to pray, to be aware of God's presence, and to find joy in him. In 1979, the Neighborhood Renewal Ministry came to St. Augustine's parish.

When the Core Team discerned Gene's potential as an evangelizer not only in St. Augustine's parish but also on the diocesan level, we invited Gene to continue the work as part of the Renewal Core Team. He willingly accepted.

Gene says:

The Parish Neighborhood Renewal Ministry has become the vehicle through which I have been fulfilled. It provided the structure through which I can be a witness and evangelize. I now understand that all that has occurred in my past life led up to this ministry. I thank God that he has placed in my heart that constant urge to listen and to hear his call.

As Jesus called forth a Peter, a James, an Andrew, and a John to be "fishers of men," so is the Renewal Core Team calling forth these modern day evangelizers: a Clarence, a Lois, a Gene, and a you.

THE BASIS

CHAPTER THREE

Prayer Paves the Way
for Parish Neighborhood Renewal

Prayer for All Believers

"I do not pray for them alone.
I pray also for those who will believe in me through
    their word,
that all may be one
as you, Father, are in me, and I in you;
I pray that they may be [one] in us,
that the world may believe that you sent me.
I have given them the glory you gave me
that they may be one, as we are one—
I living in them, you living in me—
that their unity may be complete.
So shall the world know that you sent me,
and that you loved them as you loved me."

—John 17:20-23

When I am asked, "What is the first step in parish renewal?" I always answer, "Get the whole parish to pray for renewal!" The Parish Neighborhood Renewal Ministry team encourages a prayer preparation of six months or more by calling on all the parishioners to pray for that span of time for the renewal of their parish. The parish chooses a special parish renewal prayer to be said at all parish meetings, at Mass, and at times of individual prayer. Thus renewal preparation becomes a conscious act on the part of all parishioners.

This communal action of asking the Father to send the Holy Spirit becomes ultimately an act of parish faith. Jesus has promised us results: "So I say to you, 'Ask and you shall receive; seek and you shall find; knock and it shall be opened to you'" (Luke 11:9). God does not lie! God answers prayer. I have seen how God prepares the hearts of the people for his coming in power. My people in Chile taught me the reality of this principle.

On February 23, 1956, I arrived in Licantén, Chile, a country town located in the midst of the coastal mountain range. This was to be my home for the next eleven and one-half years. It was a page out of the wild West at the end of the nineteenth century—I was met by horseback riders with pistols on their hips! However, I felt I was ready to encounter these new people of mine: I arrived well prepared with the latest techniques of evangelization and filled with the zeal of a newly-ordained priest. I discovered that I still had much to learn.

One area of my growth was in my personal relationship with God. My people taught me that God answers prayers. In theory I believed this, but in practice I wasn't so sure, at least not in the way they were. My people worked on a quid pro quo basis. "If you do this for me, Lord, I will do that for you." These bargains are called *mandas* in Chilean Spanish. I can remember telling the people not to make bargains with the Lord; that God doesn't work that way. They would smile at me and say, "Yes, Father," and then a few days later I'd see them lighting their candles of thanksgiving or bringing a gift to me for the Church—and they would say, "The Lord heard my prayer. I *won* the bargain." These people did not have all the terminology right, but they certainly knew that God answers prayer. They knew that God is faithful to his word.

The people of my parish in Licantén proved that to me in 1965 when I was a very special beneficiary of their prayers. A team of six university doctors in Santiago, Chile, diagnosed that I had a massive tumor in the upper stomach area that was in all probability cancerous. My highly irritated stomach area had many lesions. Because of the sensitivity of the area and the possibility of uncontrolled bleeding, these doctors did not perform a biopsy. Instead, they advised my superiors to send me immediately to the United States for special medical treatment. I agreed to leave Chile, but first I returned to my parish in Licantén for two days to say good-bye. I was given a beautiful send-off. I left for New York with the prayers and tears of my people beseeching heaven on my behalf.

Two weeks later, after ten days in hospitals where I underwent a battery of tests, no evidence was found of cancer, tumor, or lesions. I feel that God had certainly heard the prayers of my Chilean friends.

Acknowledging the principle that God indeed answers prayers, we advise any parish preparing for the Parish Neighborhood Renewal Ministry work to storm heaven in prayer. In these renewal prayers we ask that the Father send an outpouring of his Spirit on the parish. As Pope John XXIII asked for a New Pentecost to flow upon the universal Church, so the parish asks for the grace of Pentecost to flow upon its people.

Prayer: The Center of Renewal

The Neighborhood Renewal Ministry Core Team relies upon the promise of Jesus Christ that "if two of you join your voices on earth to pray for anything whatever, it shall be granted you by my Father in heaven" (Matthew 18:19).

When the Parish Neighborhood Renewal Ministry finished the initial work period in Holy Angels Parish, Father Robert Voigt, the pastor, was asked to give his impressions. He wrote, "I felt great power when your team prayed together. I was impressed by how you expected results from prayer." Father Voigt, who customarily starts his day with an hour of prayer, added, "I have resolved to spend even more time in prayer and especially to pray together with others."

The Renewal Core Team, recognizing our dependence on God, bases its entire apostolate on prayer. The lifestyle agreement of our evangelization community states: "Our apostolate is based on prayer and leads forth from it, principally in assisting in the establishment of Neighborhood Church Communities" (*Life-Style Agreement of the Parish Neighborhood Renewal Ministry Core Team,* #1; see Appendix A).

The demands of this growing Parish Neighborhood Renewal Ministry call us to divide ourselves into teams of two. Because of the time we must spend apart, we find a need to rejuvenate our community life. Once every three months, the Renewal Core Team comes together for an entire week to live a lifestyle of deep prayer and mutual Christian concern. During the rest of the time, each team adapts the Core Team's community lifestyle to the mission work schedule.

A prayerful lifestyle doesn't stop with us; we pass this mode of living on to those working with us in renewal. The Renewal Core Team invites the parish staff and the whole parish to experience the power of united prayer with us. One parish priest from the Duluth diocese was asked, "What excites you about Parish Neighborhood Renewal Ministry?" He responded, "It's the dimension of prayer involved. Neighborhood Renewal meets a spiritual hunger in people. People meet to pray each week on the mission for five days. They openly share their faith." He summed up his feelings by saying that during the mission, "The spiritual growth of the people from the first to the last night was exciting."

Our Renewal Core Team recommends to the parish staff that we share one hour of prime time in scriptural prayer each day. We follow a system of using four scriptural readings if time permits. We read one chapter from an Old Testament historical book, one from a prophetical or sapiential book, one psalm, and one chapter from the New Testament. After each reading we prayerfully apply the message to our daily lives. The next day we resume each reading where we left off. Spontaneous community prayer is a departure from most parish schedules. Often we hear a staff member complain, "But I have so much to do!" At this point our only reply is, "Try it; you'll like it!" As weeks go by, we notice the staff becoming comfortable with group prayer time. More than that, they see changes in those around them. They witness parishioners change from being indifferent to being enthusiastic about religion; from being bored to being interested in Sunday sermons, from being infrequent people of prayer to becoming daily Bible readers. As one staff member expressed it: "It's awesome to witness the responsiveness of people because of the mission. They're willing to cooperate. There's personal edification and close relationship with the Lord."

Since the grace of renewal is spiritual, prayer is the starting point for parish renewal. So we seek out or establish an intercessory prayer group. Such a group of laypersons brings a powerful presence of God to a parish. This group prays for renewal of the parish, for the needs of the parishioners, and for the pastor and parish staff.

The Renewal Core Team calls such a group formed for parish renewal the "prayer and teaching group." The teaching portion, presented by the Renewal Core Team, is drawn from the Vatican II Council documents that form the basis of church renewal. Other pertinent or contemporary spiritual topics are included to deepen the spiritual life of the group. However, our experience with the renewal ministry has shown that prayer is more important than talking about renewal in an intellectual way. For example, in one parish I asked the "prayer and teaching group" if they would like to continue meeting once a week for intercessory prayer. One woman said, "Do you realize that all the intentions we've prayed for over the past five weeks have been answered?" She then recounted how God had answered the prayers of the group. All were amazed and deeply edified. There was no hesitation: The group unanimously agreed to continue.

Our Renewal Core Team finds that parishioners who join with us in the renewal quickly grasp and accept an expectant, thankful, and praise-filled attitude of prayer. The hardest part is to start them praying together. Before our Renewal Core Team begins a meeting, goes out to evangelize, or makes a decision, we ask Jesus to help us, we thank him for his help, and we praise God for hearing and honoring these prayers.

One afternoon at Holy Rosary Cathedral parish, we saw the power of prayer. Our task was overwhelming us. We had an unusually large number of homes to visit because our mission was double-scheduled. Moreoever, because we were short on time, we were hurrying to complete these visits. Yet during the prayer preparation we found that two of the volunteers were feeling heavy personal burdens. The Renewal Core Team believes that we must be at peace ourselves in order not to lay our burdens on others. So instead of sending out hurting people to bring the Good News of Jesus, we opted to spend all the time necessary in prayer so that God would lift their burdens and bring them inner peace. That day we took about half the available time ministering to our hurting members. Once we finally began the home visiting late in the afternoon, we were very successful. Nevertheless, we were still behind in our visiting schedule. At the team meeting the next morning there was some skepticism about our ability to complete the visiting on time. We placed the problem in God's hands. That afternoon not only did we have more volunteers than expected, but to our amazement practically everyone on the visiting list was home. I felt that our time spent in prayer had been a wise investment.

The Gospels show that prayer was an integral part of Jesus' daily living. He prayed for guidance, especially before every important decision. Now he calls us to "come follow me" and "learn from me, for I am gentle and humble of heart" (Matthew 11:29). Our Renewal Core Team hears this call of Jesus and tries to follow him. Only through prayer can we possibly succeed.

CHAPTER FOUR

Beginning Evangelization: The Laity's Initial Role

The Basic Christian Community is a model of Church which can at once meet the individual spiritual needs of modern men and women as well as help them face being Church in the world. It is more than a way of reviving the parish; it is a way of reviving faith commitments.

—Thomas Payton, MM,
Developing Basic Christian Communities:
A Handbook, p. 40

Renewal calls us to look inward and to reach outward at the same time. Jesus taught us this basic tenet of our faith: "This is the first [commandment]: . . . 'You shall love the Lord your God with all your heart, with all your soul, with all your mind, and with all your strength.' This is the second, 'You shall love your neighbor as yourself'" (Mark 12:29-31).

Our Renewal Core Team starts with the premise that each one of us needs to be evangelized repeatedly. God asks for a continual turning toward him—in other words, a personal conversion experience requiring continual growth in openness to the Holy Spirit. This call to conversion goes out to priests, sisters, and committed laity. Such spiritual growth is supported by fellow evangelizers serving the neighborhood Church. All renewal begins with the individual, with me, but I cannot evangelize myself without the help of others. I need an affirmative community in which to live a Christian life and to become evangelized.

Moreover, because evangelization calls for this fundamental conversion experience, the formation of neighborhood Church or of Basic Church Communities is not just a passing movement but initiates a permanent renewal of church life. The ongoing evangelization spreads from the seeds of church community that are planted in each neighborhood.

One far-reaching change in the Church since Vatican II is the renewed emphasis on the laity's role in the process of evangelization. The layperson is now called upon to take active responsibility for evangelizing the world: Evangelization is a task not only for missionaries but for every Christian. Bishops, priests, sisters, parish staffs, and all laypersons need to understand this principle as reestablished by Vatican II:

> The laity derive the right and duty with respect to the apostolate from their union with Christ their Head . . . they are assigned to the apostolate by the Lord himself. They are consecrated into a royal priesthood and a holy people . . . in order that they may offer spiritual sacrifices through everything they do, and may witness to Christ throughout the world.
>
> —*Documents of Vatican II*, "Decree on the Apostolate of the Laity," paragraph 3

> The laity . . . share in the priestly, prophetic and royal office of Christ and therefore have their own role to play in the mission of the whole People of God in the Church and in the world. . . . They exercise a genuine apostolate by their activity on behalf of bringing the gospel and holiness to men; and on behalf of penetrating and perfecting the temporal sphere of things through the Spirit of the gospel. In this way, their temporal activity can openly bear witness to Christ and promote the salvation of men.
>
> —*Documents of Vatican II*, "Decree on the Apostolate of the Laity," paragraph 2

Responsible laity will be attracted to service in the renewed Church if they see that their participation is taken seriously. The

Parish Neighborhood Renewal Ministry upholds the new role of
the laity and recognizes that the neighborhood Church is pri-
marily a lay activity. (Two members of our Core Team Evangelization Community, for example, are lay persons.)

The laity's role does not diminish the priest's part in evangelization. Rather, it incorporates an untapped reservoir of power for
Christ. The Council Fathers say in their document on priests:

> To the degree of their authority and in the name of their
> bishop, priests exercise the office of Christ the Head and
> the Shepherd. Thus they gather God's family together as a
> brotherhood of living unity, and lead it through Christ and in
> the Spirit to God the Father.
> —*Documents of Vatican II*, "Decree on the
> Ministry and Life of Priests," paragraph 6

I can remember a group of laity asking Bishop Paul Anderson,
"What can we do if the pastor doesn't want to move toward parish
renewal which is the goal of the Neighborhood Renewal Ministry?
What do we do if he doesn't understand the new role of the laity?"

Bishop Anderson replied, "The role of the laity as stated in the
documents of Vatican II flows from their baptismal commitment
as sons or daughters of God. We must remember, however, that
it is not laity versus clergy, but laity and clergy working, praying,
supporting, affirming one another and moving in union with Jesus
toward the Kingdom. Lay people must constantly pray for their
priests and bishops in order that, together, all become the
Church that builds the Kingdom of God on earth."

This dialogue illustrates how one church authority encourages
his laity to assume the full responsibilities of their vocation. It is
regrettable, however, that many laypersons do not know that
Jesus is calling them to action in his Church.

Intoducing Renewal to the Parish Laity

To supply for this lack of understanding, the Neighborhood
Renewal Ministry serves a parish by offering an initial renewal

program of six weeks, followed by a six-month consultation period. Two persons from the Renewal Core Team go out to live in the parish community; they conduct five to nine neighborhood missions during the six-week period. At the same time, the Renewal Core Team trains a committed parish mission team composed of parish staff and laity who in turn will give more neighborhood missions and extend home visiting until the whole parish has been included in the renewal.

One year after Parish Neighborhood Renewal Ministry has begun at a parish, two Core Team members return to spend three weeks in the second phase of the renewal program. This phase aims at deepening the spiritual lives of the Neighborhood Renewal leaders of the parish.

How does this whole program begin? The first step in developing the Neighborhood Renewal Ministry in the parish is to present the possibilities of it to the parish council. We believe that the parish council's backing is a necessary element for the success of the renewal. Our Renewal Core Team will gladly give a presentation in a parish if both the pastoral team and the parish council desire it, or if one group is actively interested and the other merely wants more information.

When the parish staff and the parish council have decided they want the form of renewal explained in this book, the whole parish is enrolled in the prayer preparation. The parish chooses a prayer for renewal, which all parishioners are encouraged to use.

Shortly after the actual beginning of the Parish Neighborhood Renewal program, the full concept of parish renewal through the formation of Neighborhood Church Communities can be explained at weekend Masses. The presentation can be made by the parish priests or by one of the Renewal Core Team members. During the presentation, parishioners are asked to volunteer to work in the renewal as home visitors or to offer their homes as host homes for a five-day neighborhood mission. Volunteers usually sign up after Mass. Parish-wide participation is our aim; there are no age barriers or other restrictions. We encourage young people, singles, single parents, widows, widowers, and families to participate in the preparation and in the actual renewal program. The call is for a general parish renewal, beginning in a host home.

Usually, when it becomes known that host families are necessary for renewal of the parish, various families come forward to offer their homes.

An ideal host home has the following characteristics:

1. A man is present for the whole five evenings of the mission. Men want to know that there will be other men present at a religious meeting. We feel it is important to show that religion isn't only for women. The Parish Neighborhood Renewal Ministry is a renewal of the whole Church, male and female.

2. The host family is well accepted in the neighborhood. The parish staff seeks assurance that neighbors will be psychologically comfortable going to the host home. We want to make it easy for the neighborhood to come together. Family harmony is more important than the physical comforts of the home. A normal-sized room is adequate; it is friendlier to be a little crowded than to have Texas-wide spaces. When it is crowded, some of the adults simply sit on the floor with the children.

3. The host family agrees to our operating procedures. Before a host home is accepted, two members of the mission team visit the home and pray with the family. The home is blessed and the neighborhood is offered to God. Then the operating procedures for the mission are explained. The team wants the host family to understand fully the implications of the mission and the requirements placed upon them before they accept this call from God. The mission team explains the goal of forming Church in the neighborhood and of arriving at shared Christian life.

First, the family is told that *no* refreshments are to be served. This rule avoids burdening the hostess or engendering competition between family lifestyles, and it makes it easier to keep the mission within the one and one-half hour allotted for each evening. The only exception to this rule is the final meeting, when the neighbors want to celebrate their newfound community spirit.

Another rule we adhere to is that we start and end our meetings on time. The host family is asked only that they furnish a place where neighbors can come together for one and one-half hours during five evenings and that they invite their neighbors by phone after the home visiting has been completed.

The Host Family Identifies Its Neighbors

From our Renewal Core Team's experience, we know that neighborhood boundaries are not arbitrary areas on a map. Rather, they connect people with people. We ask the host family, as part of the neighborhood, to outline the neighborhood boundaries. (Since neighborhoods have definite flows of movement and common points of identification, we ask the host family for this kind of information.) Together with the host family, the Core Team determines the final size of the mission neighborhood. We suggest that approximately forty Catholic families be included in such a neighborhood. It is the Core Team's experience that between one-fourth and one-half of those families invited will attend the mission sometime during the week. The average attendance each night will be ten to twenty adults plus some children.

In selecting the first neighborhood, we take special care to choose a neighborhood that is friendly to renewal. People who are receptive to renewal at this first mission will be a source of future parish mission team members. Psychologically, a successful first mission helps the parish accept the Parish Neighborhood Renewal program.

Once the parish staff has selected a host family and that family in turn has identified its neighbors, then home visiting begins.

THE PROCESS

CHAPTER FIVE

The Home-Visiting Ministry

The Lord appointed a further seventy-two and sent them in pairs before him to every town and place he intended to visit. . . . "On entering any house, first say, 'Peace to this house.' If there is a peaceable man there, your peace will rest on him; if not, it will come back to you. . . . Into whatever city you go, after they welcome you . . . cure the sick there. Say to them, 'The reign of God is at hand.'"
—Luke 10:1-2, 5-6, 8-9

Sending parishioners out two by two in home visitation is a modern development of Jesus' sending forth the seventy-two disciples. Today Jesus still sends out disciples with his blessing. In his name and by his grace they open doors and prepare the way for him to enter neighborhoods more fully.

But the early days weren't easy. When the Parish Neighborhood Renewal Team began forming Basic Church Communities in North America, the work wasn't a big success. After our first Parish Neighborhood Renewal Ministry attempt, we recognized a difficulty in calling the neighborhood together. We were using the method we had found practical in our South American experience: There, we could get a crowd by announcing a neighborhood mission and having the host family invite their neighbors. But it didn't work so automatically in the United States. Americans seem to be more reserved than Latin Americans in religious matters. We also found that many Catholics did not know the nearby Catholic families and were hesitant about visiting a family home without a personal invitation.

As I mentioned in Chapknow the nearby Catholic families and were hesitant about visiting a family home without a personal invitation.

As I mentioned in Chapter 1, it was Sister Joan Gerads who made the breakthrough on the way to invite Americans to neighborhood missions. She drew on her missionary experience and her sociological background to develop the method that proved to work. We call it "the two-by-two home-visiting ministry." From that time on, the whole response to the neighborhood mission changed to one of open acceptance.

Looking back on those first experiences in North America, we can see how God led the Renewal Core Team to a richer and deeper ministry by use of the Home-Visiting Team. In our visits we found that God wants people to know he loves them. Just the fact that someone comes and announces the Good News of the gospel to a family shows that God loves them. God blesses the family and the home in a special way when the Home-Visiting Team prays a blessing on them. God hears the prayers offered for the family's needs and for the renewal of the neighborhood and parish. The visit opens the hearts of the family members to a conversion experience that will come through the neighborhood mission.

This may sound very simple on paper, but I can remember the first time we used the home-visiting technique. My knees were shaking as we approached the house. I kept thinking, "What will people think of our asking a blessing on their home? What will we talk about? Will they shut the door in our faces?" But then the door opened and my partner introduced us. We were graciously and joyfully received. Jesus had preceded us to the door and had entered with us! To our relief, we found the family very open to home visitation.

Many people, in fact, look forward to the visit made to their home in the name of the parish and are disappointed if they are missed. It is a rarity that the visit is rejected—perhaps once or twice in a hundred visits, our figures show. The most common response is, "Thank God! It's great to see Catholics visiting homes today. Thanks so much for praying with us!"

Lay people on the team are often confronted by the question: "How can a lay person bless a house? Isn't that the job for a priest?" I answer this by saying that only *God* blesses; neither the priest nor the lay person can bless in his or her own name. St. Peter in Acts 4:12 answers this in referring to Jesus Christ: "There is no salvation in anyone else, for there is no other name in the whole world . . . by which we are to be saved." And Jesus himself tells us, "Ask, and you will receive" (Matthew 7:7). So we ask God's blessings on the family we visit in the same way we ask God to bless our food, our safe trip, and our own family. I have always admired my brother John's family practice of having each child come to Dad for his nightly blessing. If dads or mothers can do it, so can other lay persons on home visits.

Preparation for Going Out Two by Two

As I stated earlier, when we begin the Neighborhood Renewal Ministry in a parish, we ask for home-visiting volunteers. At our first meeting with the volunteers, we devote the first half hour to shared prayer. We pray for the teams going forth and for the families to be visited. Usually, to help us in prayer, we read some Scripture such as the passage quoted at the beginning of this chapter. That account of Jesus' sending forth the seventy-two disciples challenges the group.

Jesus Christ is the one who changes lives. Nonetheless, he uses us as instruments to touch others. Part of the preparation for home visiting is learning the techniques to make us better instruments, and one of the ways of our teaching these techniques is to "walk through" a typical visit, giving the lay volunteers an opportunity for questions and answers.

Another purpose of this initial meeting is to relax those about to make home visits and to reassure them of God's presence in this mission. We explain that God always seems to get the right people to the right house. Lay people are often surprised to find that God can use their life experiences to help people who are passing through some of the same trials as they are.

In summary, then, our Renewal Core Team explains to the new volunteers what God accomplishes during a home visit. Then through a model dialogue, we present the technique to use. We assure our volunteers that each of them will be accompanied by an experienced home visitor. This policy presents a personnel challenge to our small Renewal Core Team. We solve this problem by calling on volunteer home visitors from nearby parishes where the Parish Neighborhood Renewal Ministry is underway. These volunteers help us form the initial teams and train the new parish home visitors.

For example, we called for experienced home visitors to help us in the rural parish of Floodwood, Minnesota. It was late November, and four inches of fresh snow covered the ground. Despite Sunday afternoon football mania, some fifty volunteers arrived to assist in home visiting. They had come from as far as forty to fifty miles away. We divided into two groups: one to pray for successful visiting, the other to make the home visits. At the spaghetti dinner afterward, these volunteers expressed their joy because they had been able to bring the warmth of God's blessing into over one-half of the homes of this rural parish.

The Technique of Home Visiting

We go forth two by two prayerfully and with a deep sense of mission. If any member of the team is feeling ill, burdened, or irritable, we pray with this person first so that the love of God will flow through him or her. We are very conscious of the presence of Jesus in each one of us.

We have prayed as a group, and then we pray as two of us go from family to family. We find that where it is possible, it is more effective to form mixed teams. The man-woman balance, and especially the husband-wife team, is very effective. We go about the neighborhood on foot, blessing the physical setting and all persons we encounter. Our primary purpose is to bring Jesus to those we meet, to shower them with his love, peace, blessings, and joy.

The secondary purpose of home visiting is to invite the families to the neighborhood mission. But it is important to keep this invitation in its proper perspective: The primary aspect of home visiting is the blessing of the home and the ensuing prayer.

In our technique of visiting, we alternate our speaking. While one team member speaks, the other will be praying that God will bless the visit. Each visit is different, of course, so any guidelines we give should be adapted to the situation. Nothing should be too rigid.

A typical visit begins with the first visitor greeting a family member: "Good afternoon. This is Mary Smith and I'm Bill Jones. We're home-visiting from St. Mary's parish. May we come in and pray a blessing on your home?" Usually the visiting team is invited in immediately. The second team member then prays that the peace of Jesus will come upon the family and the home. Home visitors pray for all the family needs they can observe as well as for its protection from sickness, disasters, scandal, and disunity. They ask that God will always dwell within that family unit.

Upon finishing this home-blessing prayer, the first visitor then asks if the family would like everyone present to join in prayer for any special needs or family intentions. This invitation reminds them that their prayer, too, is heard by God. If the family has no stated intentions and says that everyting is fine, we say a prayer of thanksgiving for God's love for them.

The second visitor then distributes copies of the parish-renewal prayer and leads the group in praying it. We leave enough copies of the prayer for the family and ask them to say it daily. On the bottom of one prayer sheet is an invitation to the neighborhood mission. Here is a sample:

You are invited to attend a neighborhood mission to begin on Monday, March 5, from 7:30 P.M. to 9:00 P.M. Sharp! At the home of Jim and Pat Brown, 135 Walnut Street. The mission will continue for five evenings and will close with a home Mass. Come with your whole family.

The other team member briefly explains the invitation to join the neighborhood mission. He or she answers any questions and urges the family to make a real effort to come the first night of the mission. He or she tells them the mission is a good opportunity for them to meet their Catholic neighbors. Our Core Team recommends emphasizing "the first night billing" of the Neighborhood Mission because most lay people need to grow into the five-night commitment. After their first night's exposure, the Lord seems to help most of these "first-nighters" to clear their weekly calendar for the renewal experience.

Our goal is to visit all the Catholic families in the neighborhood, whether or not they are on a parish list or even belong to any parish or have stopped the formal practice of their religion. With this goal in mind, the visitors ask the family to identify other Catholic families nearby. Through home visits, our Renewal Core Team usually discovers three or four nonpracticing Catholic families; sometimes the visit is the start of a reconciliation with God. One woman gave public testimony at her neighborhood mission, describing how the visit to her home brought her back to the Church and sacraments after fifteen years. When Christians have the courage to step out into the neighborhood on Christ's behalf, his grace follows with abundance!

Our Renewal Core Team advises beginning a Parish Neighborhood Renewal program with those families in which one or both partners are Catholic. This does not mean that we look down at our Protestant neighbors, but that we find many Catholics are not acquainted or comfortable with even their Catholic neighbors. To invite their Protestant friends before there is a community feeling among the Catholics changes the dynamics of the group. The goal, after all, is for Catholics to become a neighborhood church community.

More Voices

The seventy-two returned in jubilation. . . . [Jesus said,] "See what I have done; I have given you power. . . .

Nevertheless, do not rejoice so much in the fact that devils
are subject to you as that your names are inscribed in
heaven."

—Luke 10:17-20

Modern-day disciples are experiencing the jubilation of Jesus'
time through the Home-Visiting Ministry. God's grace touches
both the visitor and the family visited. Here are some examples of
how God's Good News has changed lives and has given great
satisfaction to those participating in this ministry.

One of our home visitors received a phone call from a person
who had been visited the previous day. "Mary Ann," the voice
said, "I just want you to know that when you and Father Jim
prayed in our home, I had a real sense of God's presence. I slept
very peacefully last night, and this morning, even before I was
fully awake, I just knew that God had to be more in my life." As
she hung up the receiver, Mary Ann felt a warm glow inside
herself. Later she told us how thrilled she was that the Holy Spirit
was using her.

One older man who hadn't been attending church promised,
after the visit to his home, to come every night to the mission. He
fulfilled his word, and God truly touched him.

Father Jim Crossman relates that one person who had rejected
the home-visiting team started going to Mass again. Even this
apparent failure became a conversion experience.

And from the "other side of the neighborhood's doors" came
this comment from one home visitor: "I was amazed to find that
every family we visited asked for prayers over some problem."
She said she then realized her own problems were not unique;
with Jesus and prayer, her life had new meaning.

CHAPTER SIX

Experiencing
the Neighborhood Mission

You . . . are "a chosen race, a royal priesthood, a holy nation, a people he claims for his own to proclaim the glorious works" of the One who called you from darkness into his marvelous light. Once you were no people, but now you are God's people; once there was no mercy for you, but now you have found mercy.

—1 Peter 2:9-10

Once the neighborhood doors are opened through home visiting, the way is paved for the next step toward renewal: the neighborhood mission. Usually during the week after the home visiting, another committed group, the mission team, prepares to hold a five-night neighborhood mission. Initially, two Renewal Core Team members serve on a parish mission team comprised of priests, sisters, and laity. The laity includes teenagers as well as adults who will participate in each neighborhood mission within their parish. But the Renewal Core Team cautions that no more than six persons on the parish mission team should come into a neighborhood mission. Too many mission team members can prevent the feeling of closeness from developing among neighbors.

Deeply committed to prayer, this mission team meets each evening before the scheduled mission to pray for themselves and for the mission participants.

The period of home visiting prior to the neighborhood mission seems to build anticipation within a neighborhood group—almost like Advent's preparation for Christmas. Most neighborhoods sponsor few group activities, so the home visits build up interest in the mission. A few minutes before the mission begins, people leave their homes to walk over to the host home. In these times it is a rare sight to see families out walking in the evening to visit a neighbor. Thus the whole neighborhood becomes more aware of the mission gathering. People begin to ask, "What's going on at So-and-so's?"

The actual place for the mission is determined by the host family. Just about any place is suitable, depending on weather and space limitations. The physical setting is chosen for the convenience of those participating. Common areas used in our work have been living rooms and recreation rooms. Backyards, patios, and garages are also possibilities, but we do not choose the parish church or neighborhood chapels, because we invite some non-practicing Catholics who might find it difficult to go into a formal church situation. Our meeting style is informal and nonthreatening.

The host family selects a time that will be most convenient for the other families in the neighborhood. The mission team always tries to accommodate itself to the neighborhood time schedule.

God wants his people to enjoy being with one another, so the meeting should begin with an easy ambience among the neighbors. To start off in harmony, the team teaches the group a few simple, spirited songs in praise of God. (St. Augustine reminds us that to sing in praise of God is to pray twice.) The mission team plans the meeting so that there is an even distribution of time between presentations and prayer. During prayer time, the team members help the neighbors in praying out loud. Everything is done in a spirit of prayer in order to be mindful of the Holy Spirit working in the heart of each person present. Participants experience a powerful personal involvement in the mission, and at the same time they feel the thrust of coming together as a neighborhood. They begin sharing life together as intimate Christian friends will, and it takes only one or two nights for a spirit of joy and good feeling to emerge in the group.

The thrust of the mission is basic evangelization that brings each person into contact with Jesus and his word. Each presentation begins with a scripture text followed by the speaker's reflections. Often we ask those present to share what they have received as the principal message. Confident that the Word of God is more important than the word of any other person, the mission team tries to present Jesus to the group, allowing him to touch their hearts.

During the teaching or testimony of a team member, the other team members are praying that God will use this moment to touch the hearts of those listening. They call on God's power to make the mission effective.

To help bring each person to a conversion experience, the mission presents a basic evangelization theme that I like to call a "walk with Jesus." In well-prepared steps the mission draws a person to reflect upon God's personal love for him or her. That person will feel Jesus' concern for the sick, will hear Jesus saying that he or she is the temple of the Holy Spirit and that he or she can unite with others in the Holy Spirit to pray for family and friends who are ailing. Each person is invited to accept Jesus into his or her life as friend and Lord.

Our Core Team always seeks out and trains new lay members for the mission team. The first participation of a new member at the mission would ordinarily be to relate how God touched him or her at a previous mission. We expect the conversion that grew out of the mission to motivate the person to share it with others. Those who hear this testimony are often deeply edified. This sharing also helps the team member since it publicly reaffirms his or her commitment to God. If the Renewal Core Team observes that the person has the gift of teaching, he or she will next be asked to share a reflection on a scriptural passage. Because he or she is gradually brought into the team's ministry role, the new member gains the confidence eventually to give one of the basic evangelistic teachings on a mission.

Each night of the mission, the participants are encouraged to entrust to Jesus the needs of family, friends, and self. To visualize this handing over of personal intentions, we ask them to imagine

Jesus standing in the group with a large basket in his hands, collecting the petitions of the group. Frequently these prayers are answered. One participant says, "I thank God for healing my back. I asked for the prayers of our group and the pain disappeared. It's a real blessing!" Many participants experience healings, spiritual and physical, during this week of deep prayer. Each evening, time is also set aside to thank God for the blessings experienced during the day.

The First Goal of the Mission:
Personal Conversion

The acceptance of Jesus and of the Holy Spirit is a deeply personal experience, similar to the coming of the Holy Spirit to the disciples on Pentecost. Participants often feel great joy and peace. Occasionally, though, they seem to experience nothing except knowing that they are not the same as before. Today in all parts of the world the Church is feeling the power of renewal in the Holy Spirit. It seems to be the answer to the prayer of Pope John XXIII, who asked for a present-day Pentecost.

One member of the neighborhood mission group tells how her family experienced a renewal in the Spirit:

> We were a host family in the neighborhood. Our family benefited from this experience and from the Neighborhood Renewal Group that we have formed now. Our family is more united in religion. God was always important in our home, but now he is emphasized even more. I myself feel more comfortable telling my family about faith experiences.

She added, "Prayer has more meaning to us. Our teenage daughter says her faith has deepened—it's more than 'just something learned as a kid.'" She concluded that "getting to know our neighbors better means that we are more aware of their needs and can pray for them."

Her husband says:

I agree that we have seen a deepening of our faith and the faith of the other members of our group through the mission and the meetings. This is evident when we have our group sharing time. Just about everyone at these meetings has an example of God's workings. Speaking for myself, I can see where my faith has grown. Before all this took place and when I was in need of something, prayer was my last resort. Now when I have a problem, big or small, prayer is the first thought that comes to mind.

He added, "I have also learned to realize that there always is an answer to my prayers, although it might not be the one I was expecting."

He shared his belief, too, that

the best thing that actually happened to me took place the first week of the mission. I was changed by the Holy Spirit! It really was an experience I will always remember. I was filled with peace and joy, and I still am, although not always to that extent. I know it carries over at work. A number of people have commented that I seem happier with my job.

Then he confided, "I think it might be rubbing off on some of my coworkers; one in particular has cleaned up his language since I found the courage to tell him off. It may be just a small incident, but it's a start."

The neighborhood celebrates the closing night of the mission in the context of a home Mass. We offer to God the experiences of the five evenings, together with the hopes, needs, and thanks of each one present. The whole neighborhood is held up to God for blessing. The Mass is a celebration of community—a community that becomes a neighborhood reality.

The Second Goal of the Mission:
Formation of Community

The mission team concludes the fifth evening by asking the people, "How many of you would like to continue meeting

together?" Usually there is an excellent response. The team then
explains both the need for a small number of people to coordinate
the meetings and the way of selecting these "servant-leaders."
We find the name "servant-leader" is very expressive of the role
of these coordinators. Father Pat Okada, a Benedictine priest,
told us how he interprets "servant-leader":

> It's a very Christian title and it's new. It's like the cross, a
> contradiction—servant plus leader. It makes people ask
> why you call them that, and you can explain what you mean.
> It's a new work of the Church and should have a new name.

The neighborhood community chooses its servant-leaders
under the guidance of the Holy Spirit. All present are invited to
enter into deep prayer of praise and love of God. They ask the
Holy Spirit to give them the names of three or four servant-
leaders as they pray in silence. The Renewal Core Team suggests
that the group retain at least two men to be named first as
servant-leaders to assure ongoing male participation. At the end
of the deep prayer, the mission team leader asks if anyone in the
community has felt God suggesting a name to him or her. After
three or four names have surfaced, each person named is asked if
he or she will accept to serve the group in the name of Jesus.
Acceptance is easier if one knows the other people who will be
asked to be servant-leaders. Also experience teaches us that we
should always invite the men first. When a person is named, he or
she is free to say, "Yes, I accept to serve the group in Jesus'
name," or "No, I am not able to do so at this time." Each servant-
leader should freely choose and not be pressured into accepting.
Limiting the length of office to one year may make acceptance
easier.

As a final act of the Mass, the whole group gathers around to
place hands on the servant-leaders and to ask God's blessings on
them. In this blessing God is asked to give the new servant-
leaders and the whole group the gifts of the Holy Spirit necessary
for their new church community. These gifts of the Holy Spirit
are intended first for the building up of the community and then
for the extending out in service to the neighborhood at large.

After the blessing, the newly chosen servant-leaders meet to decide the place, date, and time of the next Neighborhood Renewal group meeting. This information is then immediately announced so that the Neighborhood Church Community will begin functioning without delay.

The Neighborhood Church Community plants a seed of Christian life among neighbors. Its goal is not to form a prayer group, but rather to share Christian life. The Renewal Core Team encourages the group not to focus on numbers but on the seed of God's presence. Even if only a few come together on a regular basis at first, they will grow in their faith, the neighborhood will benefit, and God will give the increase.

Jesus said that the seed that fell on good soil and yielded grain "sprang up to produce at a rate of thirty- and sixty- and a hundredfold." The seed is those "who listen to the word [and] take it to heart" (Mark 4:8, 20).

CHAPTER SEVEN

Renewal Touches Parishioners and Pastor Alike

We keep thanking God for all of you and we remember you
in our prayers, for we constantly are mindful before our God
and Father of the way you are proving your faith, and
laboring in love, and showing constancy of hope in our Lord
Jesus Christ. We know, too, . . . beloved of God, how you
were chosen. Our preaching of the gospel proved not a
mere matter of words for you but one of power; it was
carried on in the Holy Spirit and out of complete conviction.
—1 Thessalonians 1:2-5

Our goal with the neighborhood mission is to help form and then
leave a community empowered by the Holy Spirit to continue
sharing Christian life. In short, the Parish Neighborhood Renewal
Ministry is not a "one-shot experience" of God's love and presence. This new community is encouraged to meet frequently,
once a week if possible. The Renewal Core Team, drawing on its
North American experience, suggests that for consistently spirited meetings, the servant-leaders should meet before each
meeting to pray and plan.

There is a good reason for choosing more than one servant-
leader: When one servant-leader must miss a meeting, there is
still sufficient leadership to continue. Weekly meetings are rec-
ommended so that should a person miss one meeting, there will
be only a two-week gap in his or her contact with neighbors. A

word of caution: If the meetings are scheduled two weeks or three weeks apart, the interval lengthens into a month or six weeks between meetings for the person who misses a meeting. This defeats the purpose of coming together, since a community needs frequent contact to deepen and grow.

Each Neighborhood Church Community is free to choose its format provided that two basic elements are present: group prayer and life- and faith-sharing. First, in prayer the group recognizes and gives thanks for the way God is working in the neighborhood. Also, the members allot time for the prayer of petition. Most groups include sharing of Scripture. Second, to address the life- and faith-sharing aspects, each group shares its daily joys and problems. Together the members examine and find solutions for the group's need to grow in love and active concern for one another and for the neighborhood's need to become more livable through the outreach of these people who form a nucleus of Neighborhood Church. They also enjoy sharing events such as marriage anniversaries, birthdays, liturgical feasts, and national holidays.

Our Renewal Core Team finds that most Neighborhood Church Communities look forward to their weekly sharing. The most common complaint is that the meetings end too quickly. Jan Hannig finds her neighborhood meeting a very special event. The group senses something of the Spirit's presence at each get-together. Jan says, "It is really special to experience the Holy Spirit at work at our meetings." The Hannigs and the other leader couple meet before their group meeting to go over different scriptural or other spiritual readings. Jan explains, "Somehow, during the meeting the Holy Spirit seems to blend it all together so that it's all appropriate for the meeting."

Jan's husband Rich describes how their faith community has developed:

The best part of our neighborhood group meeting is the sharing time. I think we were all a little bit timid at first about putting our problems in the basket held by Jesus; but now, with a year under our belts, we're much freer. Now we're bringing the problems of others along with our own. We have much to be thankful about now. You can feel the neighbors responding when another member shares something good that happened to them.

Most Neighborhood Church Communities find that in the beginning a one-hour meeting is sufficient. The participants must first be comfortable with one another; then they can decide what length of meeting is best for them. Our experience is that in time a group will define its identity; but if the early meetings become too lengthy, many members will drop out.

The Pastor and the Neighborhood Church Community

When a parish opts to form a Neighborhood Church Community, the parish makes a serious commitment to support it. This renewal program is not designed to dump a whole new work load on the pastor or pastoral team. In reality, it should make their work easier as new leaders emerge within the parish. The pastor discovers a new apostolic network through which he can communicate with his people. However, for the network to be effective, the servant-leaders should meet monthly with the pastor. Frequent meetings permit a flow of information among the groups themselves and between them and the pastor.

From the beginning of the neighborhood mission, the Renewal Core Team has encouraged lay responsibility among parishioners. The monthly meeting is no exception. The lay leader who chairs this meeting will call on each Neighborhood Church Community to share its successes and failures. The other servant-leaders feel freer with a lay chairperson, and they themselves will offer solutions to problems and will share their views. The pastor is an active participant in this meeting, but his greatest gain comes from listening and observing.

The format is similar to that of a Neighborhood Church Community meeting: Time is given for Scripture sharing, thanksgiving prayer, and at the end of the meeting, for petitions. A portion of the meeting is often used for teachings on leadership skills, spiritual growth, and resource services for the neighborhood communities.

There are two dimensions to this meeting of pastor and servant-leaders. First, there is the mutual sharing and affirmation of the leadership of the groups by the members themselves. Second, the pastor both affirms the leadership of the neighborhood groups and receives a clear picture of what is happening within specific sectors of the parish.

The Pastor's Role in Neighborhood Church Renewal

The relationship between the pastor and the Neighborhood Church Community is an example of how the Church is being renewed. The pastor's role shifts from one of planning, directing, and guiding all activity of the parish to that of working with and supporting the Neighborhood Church Communities as they step forth to serve their neighbors. The renewed Church now envisions a priest's principal work as that of spiritual leadership. The priest helps his parishioners to be open to the Holy Spirit and to be aware of the workings of God. The pastor calls forth the gifts of the Spirit given to each person for the service of the community. As a guide, a priest must fulfill St. Paul's charge to the Thessalonians:

> Do not stifle the Spirit. Do not despise prophecies. Test everything; retain what is good. Avoid any semblance of evil.
>
> —1 Thessalonians 5:19-22

It is exciting for priests to see this fresh outpouring of the Spirit open up vast new areas in which they can be creative. Priests discover how to use the gifts and ministries of the laity. As the laity fulfill their true vocation of apostleship and begin to share many priestly day-to-day tasks, pastors will become freer to recognize and call forth the gifts from an ever-growing number of the laity.

I remember what happened in my own life in Chile. I had been the bishop's assistant and troubleshooter, as well as secretary general of the diocese—a hybrid chancellor-vicar general. Nothing was too small or too big for me to tackle, and I was always on the go. Then, in the midst of all this busyness, I began somehow to sense that God was telling me, "Go back to your little people." In time, God led me to ask my bishop and Maryknoll superior to allow me to return to a more spiritual, simpler lifestyle. To my delight, they granted my request.

Once I became less work-oriented, I found more time for prayer. It was a new experience for me: I became available to people, especially to help them grow spiritually. I could now identify with their desire for a deeper personal relationship with God. I can remember one person's telling me that before I changed, I was never available after the first conversation. I was too work-oriented and not enough people-oriented.

Now I can identify with St. Paul's letter to the Philippians.

> Rejoice in the Lord always! I say it again. Rejoice! Everyone should see how unselfish you are. The Lord is near. Dismiss all anxiety from your minds. Present your needs to God in every form of prayer and in petitions full of gratitude. Then God's own peace, which is beyond all understanding, will stand guard over your hearts and minds, in Christ Jesus. Finally, . . . your thoughts should be wholly directed to all that is true, all that deserves respect, all that is honest, pure, admirable, decent, virtuous, or worthy of praise.
> —Philippians 4:4-8

Besides calling priests to a deeper spirituality, the Parish Neighborhood Renewal Ministry can radically alter a priest's view of his own life. Father John Dolsina says of our renewal program, "The Parish Neighborhood Renewal Ministry has renewed my parish and my own life totally. Here I was, thinking of retirement—now it's a new beginning for me!" Father John is in his seventies, but he claims to have his youth back and is eager to be evangelizing.

Father John Doyle recognized the potential of the Parish Neighborhood Renewal Ministry for his parish. He was one of the first priests in the United States to come into contact with Parish Neighborhood Renewal Ministry. He invited the Renewal Core Team to start building faith communities in his parish in February 1978. Father Doyle, speaking as a pastor, shares his view of Parish Neighborhood Renewal:

> Several years ago, in God's great providence, I met Sister Joan and Father Tom in Bishop Anderson's kitchen in Duluth, Minnesota. After the usual introductory conversation, I learned about their neighborhood mission work in Venezuela. It seemed an excellent vehicle for building a spirit of community within neighborhoods which together formed a parish. We could become a parish family if each neighborhood had already become a united "family."
>
> At about this time our diocese was conducting a diocesan-wide survey of the people's needs and desires in preparation for Call to Action programs. The consensus of the people was that we needed help: (1) to grow in a spirit of prayer and spirituality, (2) to strengthen families, (3) to grow in a sense of community. The Parish Neighborhood Renewal Ministry seemed to be the answer to our prayers.
>
> People have really learned to pray together as a result of their mission and weekly meetings. Recently a parishioner said, "Our neighborhood is different from what it was a year ago; we've become like brothers and sisters!" When I heard this, I knew that the Parish Neighborhood Renewal Ministry was attaining its goal.

CHAPTER EIGHT

Developing Ministries
for Service

There are different gifts but the same Spirit; there are
different ministries but the same Lord; there are different
works but the same God who accomplishes all of them in
everyone. To each person the manifestation of the Spirit is
given for the *common good*. [Emphasis added.]
                                        —1 Corinthians 12:4-7

One stimulating aspect of the Parish Neighborhood Renewal
Ministry is to watch Neighborhood Church Community members grow in consciousness of their responsibility to the faith
community and to the neighborhood. Ministries of prayer, reconciliation, peacemaking, and wisdom are necessary to every faith
community. (In the various lists of gifts or ministries that appear
in the New Testament, especially in the writings of St. Paul, the
orientation is almost exclusively that of the faith community. See 1
Corinthians 12:6-11 and 12:28-31; Ephesians 4:11-13; Romans
12:6-8.)

These renewed people realize that their gifts are to serve the
common good. The Parish Neighborhood Renewal Ministry rein-
forces this call to ministry by encouraging each person in the use
of his or her gifts. In 1 Peter 4:10, the author writes, "As generous
distributors of God's manifold grace, put your gifts at the service
of one another, each in the measure he has received." This

chapter will describe some of the principles governing these ministries.

St. James tells us that true conversion requires acts of service:

> If a brother or sister has nothing to wear and no food for the day, and you say to them, "Goodbye and good luck! Keep warm and well fed," but do not meet their bodily needs, what good is that? So it is with faith that does nothing in practice. It is thoroughly lifeless.
>
> —James 2:15-17

Jesus designates the treatment of the needy and hurting as the deciding factor in whether a person will be rewarded or punished on the last day:

> "The king will say to those on his right: 'Come. You have my Father's blessing! Inherit the kingdom prepared for you from the creation of the world. For I was hungry and you gave me food, I was thirsty and you gave me drink. I was a stranger and you welcomed me, naked and you clothed me. I was ill and you comforted me, in prison and you came to visit me.' Then the just will ask him: 'Lord, when did we . . . [do this thing for you]?' The king will answer them: 'I assure you, as often as you did it for one of my least brothers, you did it for me.'"
>
> —Matthew 25:34-37, 40

In this passage Jesus promised to reward his servant people not only for giving material things, but also for welcoming, comforting, and visiting people. These little daily actions become significant in his eyes. They are works of ministry to the faith community and to the neighborhood.

The Christian, then, is called to share what he or she has. Many of us Christians focus on an immediate response to a needy brother or sister. St. Paul clearly indicates a far wider responsibility.

> Tell those who are rich in this world's goods not to be proud, and not to rely on so uncertain a thing as wealth. Let them

trust in the God who provides us richly with all things for our use. Charge them to do good, to be rich in good works and generous, *sharing what they have.* [Emphasis added.]
—1 Timothy 6:17-18

The material goods of this world are for all humans. Possessions become a barrier to the development of the faith community whenever a member tries to maintain possession of material goods to the neglect of other Christians' needs.

Another type of ministry is service to our environment. The earth and its creatures are our inheritance from God, to be used for the service of all. Each person is called to put order into the natural world. But God charged men and women to be caretakers, not owners, of creation, which is for the glory of God. A person becomes caretaker of creation by virtue of union with the Creator, through whom all creation is supported in being. "In [Jesus] everything in heaven and on earth was created. . . ; all were created through him, and for him. . . . In him everything continues in being" (Colossians 1:16-17).

As Christians contemplate their union with God, they see their responsibility for putting order into the world and preserving it in balance. Christians are to continue the work of salvation and thus assure the earth's use for generations to come.

Indeed, the whole created world eagerly awaits the revelation of the sons of God. . . . The world itself will be freed from its slavery to corruption and share in the glorious freedom of the children of God. Yes, we know that all creation groans and is in agony even until now.
—Romans 8:19, 21

Environmental responsibility is a type of religious ministry that is often overlooked and indeed frequently left to the secular disciplines of science, engineering, and politics.

General Types of Ministry

One might ask, "How many ministries are there?" The answer I would give is that the number of ministries is like the number of stars in a galaxy. The clearer and sharper our vision, the more stars we see. The clearer the Christian sees Jesus working in his or her life, the more ways he or she can see of ministering to others.

One primary method of calling forth persons into any given ministry is by means of the parish council, endorsed by the Second Vatican Council to provide a broader base for parish direction. With the pastor, this council has the authority and the privilege of instituting new ministries. One caution, however, about calling forth ministries: Ministry is not the same as busyness. A ministry must be a service for the common good and based on love. Again, while janitorial service, church decoration, parish financing, and general repair are legitimate ministries, they are not the principal thrust of a basic Christian community. Material housekeeping is not the same as spiritual ministry. Spiritual ministry is evangelizing, loving, counseling, teaching, praying, healing, and sharing—all of which are basic to the Christian vocation.

Ministries that are the faith community's outreach to the neighborhood stem from Jesus' compassion on the multitude and his charge to the Church to evangelize all peoples. Christians have a twofold service to fellow humans—to respond to both material and spiritual needs. The Church is to carry on Jesus' work in the world.

> Then [Jesus] told them: "Go into the whole world and proclaim the good news to all creation. Signs like these will accompany those who have professed their faith: they will use my name to expel demons, they will speak entirely new languages, . . .and the sick upon whom they lay their hands will recover."
>
> —Mark 16:15, 17-18

The Neighborhood Church Community must be a sign of Jesus' love to its neighbors. As Neighborhood Church it sends forth its members to serve the neighborhood in the name of Jesus. Those sent have an official, missionary ministry from the Church.

There are ministries that serve both the faith community and the neighborhood itself. In the context of the entire neighborhood community, our Renewal Core Team has witnessed the power of ministries to establish better living conditions, educational advances, safety precautions, and protection for people and nature. Potentially these ministries can extend beyond neighborhood boundaries as they show a concern for all and seek to build a community lifestyle that eliminates injustice and racial tension. Such ministries often turn neighbors' apathy into Christlike action.

The Principle of Subsidiarity

The Second Vatican Council approved and used the principle of subsidiarity. This policy simply means that actions should be done and decisions should be made by the lowest competent authority; higher authority is not to usurp the decision-making competency of lower authority.

The reason I bring the principle of subsidiarity into a chapter on ministry is that each of the different levels of Church has a need for and responsibility for ministry. Traditionally, the parish has centralized all decision-making in the pastor, thus bypassing the Churches of family and neighborhood. Since the Neighborhood Church Community is truly Church, pastors must make an effort to return decision-making to it. The ministries of the Neighborhood Church Community flow out of Neighborhood Church and form an appropriate expression of that Church.

Recently I encountered a lay person who was afraid to visit an aged parishioner because the parish had a staff parish visitor. The lay person erred on two points. First, as an individual, a Christian is called to take Jesus to anyone in need; second, as a member of a community, a Christian is called to reach out in the name of the community.

If persons are to grow in the renewed Neighborhood Church Communities, the parish must encourage neighborhood initiative: A truly renewed parish is one that fosters all ministries to serve the common good. Understanding this evangelistic momentum, the parish will seek out creative ways to identify the expanded ministries needed and suggested by its parishioners. The pastor and staff, rather than restricting certain ministries because those ministries are already functioning on a parish level, will encourage the neighborhood ministries and thus multiply the presence of Jesus. As the parish grows with additional Neighborhood Church Communities, there will be a new outreach in love and concern, and the parish will expand its vision of the Neighborhood Church Community. (In Latin America, for example, the Neighborhood Church Community prepares its members for reception of the sacraments and then celebrates those sacraments with the parish priest.)

Though each Neighborhood Church Community will have an outreach toward its neighbors, its first thrust in love and service should be toward its own members. Unless there is a deep sense of love and concern among the participants, a group will not be a Christian sign for those outside itself. As a group grows spiritually in love and unity, its power to serve others in good work will flourish. St. Paul frequently urged that the members of the community should love one another. His greatest cross was the divisions, infighting, and bad example given by the Churches he had founded. The quickest way to destroy a faith community is to divide it with envy, dissension, and mistrust. Once a Neighborhood Church Community has been established, we usually expect that it will take about a year of interior and spiritual growth before it will have strength to attract new members. While it will have some outreach, the new community needs first to find its own identity. The community arrives at its identity as deep prayer, Bible sharing, and personal sharing build up the levels of trust and love among its members. Only then will the experience of the first communities of the Acts of the Apostles be repeated today. People will be able to say of twentieth-century Christians what they said of the early Christians: "See how they love one another!"

In this chapter, I have examined the principles of ministry and how they are an essential part of the neighborhood Church. In the following chapter I will further describe the use of these ministries in bringing radical change to the neighborhood and parish.

THE RESULTS

CHAPTER NINE

Renewed Neighborhoods, Vehicles of Social Change

Jesus took the book of the prophet Isaiah and read:

"The spirit of the Lord is upon me;
   therefore he has anointed me.
He has sent me to bring glad tidings to the poor,
   to proclaim liberty to captives,
Recovery of sight to the blind
   and release to prisoners,
To announce a year of favor from the Lord."

"Today this Scripture passage is fulfilled in your hearing."
[Emphasis added.]

—Luke 4:18-19, 21

The Neighborhood Renewal Mission brings people into an evangelization experience that results in a fuller relationship with the Lord. This growth gives one changed attitudes toward one's faith and toward one's neighbor: The individual so touched feels a compelling desire to show the love that God has stirred up, and this zeal results in action. When this process of growth in the Spirit is felt by a Neighborhood Church Community, the Community frequently responds to social concerns. The Spirit helps the Community discover a new power that enables it to respond to those who are hurting: the poor, the lonely, the sick, the aged, the oppressed or weak, those in any way less rich in God's gifts.

The Neighborhood Church Community discovers how to become effective in relieving needs and in facing social issues. Moreover, the conversion experience makes its members *want* to do it. One cannot love without wanting to serve! Thus a renewed sense of responsibility bursts forth in service to the people of the neighborhood.

Concern for the Poor

Renewed persons take a deeper look at how they can share what they have with the poor and needy. They address such problems as the lack of food, shelter, clothing, medicine, and informational resources that lead to jobs, health services, and so on. Moreover, by our presence among poor people, we are able to show them compassion. These are *Christian concerns,* and all of us need to grow in them. In the United States we have often bypassed the individual Christian's need, choosing instead to "help" people by sending them to agencies of the church, city, county, or state. These same agencies at times may even discourage individual response.

An inspiring example of neighborhood concern occurred in Hibbing, Minnesota. Several winters ago, during one of the spells of extreme cold, the water pipes froze and broke in a dilapidated house where an eighty-year-old semiinvalid man lived alone with his meager possessions. He could not repair the pipes himself, and there was no response from the absentee landlord. Learning of the emergency, the Neighborhood Church Community repaired the broken pipes, fixed up the house, and took this senior citizen under its care. One of the group's families contacted the landlord and found that there was little interest either in the old man or in rehabilitating the house in which he had lived for over forty years. The result was that this same family bought the house and then assured the elderly man that he could live there as long as he wished.

Helping the Aged

Most neighborhoods have some older people who are limited in activity either by health or by lack of company to share life with them. Many will not go out alone in the evening. By reaching out to give companionship, transportation, or the opportunity to get together with their neighbors, the Neighborhood Church Community can add a richer dimension to such persons' lives and enrich the neighborhood through these contacts. Without question, older people have much to share with us if we take the time to listen. They are rich in life experience and possess a wealth of cultural and spiritual wisdom.

Providing an Environment
for Reentry into Normal Life

Patients who return home from institutions and hospitals need special love. The Neighborhood Church Community can speed their reentry into normal living by friendliness, concern, and help. Those who have experienced drug dependency, divorce proceedings, or prolonged medical care all need an affirming environment. Their self-image has often been destroyed; a caring neighborhood will help immensely in the necessary rebuilding. Some hospitals and institutions are delighted to learn that there is a local Christian group willing to reach out to these partially rehabilitated neighbors. Continued outpatient clinical counseling often counts on this support.

Caring for the Sick

Caring for the sick is one of the most obvious areas of neighborhood concern. We all understand to some degree what this entails: the actual treatment, financial help, visits, encouragement, and prayer with the sick for healing. In a less obvious way of assisting, friends and neighbors can enable the members of a family to take a welcome vacation break from the burden of caring for a chronically ill relative and thus give that family renewed strength to bear its burdens.

I am reminded of a group who responded to the needs of a family when the father was experiencing serious medical problems. The neighborhood took responsibility for the household, which allowed the wife to live with her husband at the hospital. The group assumed a multitude of family duties, from chauffeuring the children and cutting the lawn to feeding the family and doing the laundry and more. In addition, they secured financial help to pay for the high medical expenses. Simultaneously, the whole neighborhood came together in prayer for the father's healing and rapid recovery. Thanks to the catalytic effect of the Neighborhood Church Community, a family was not alone through a very difficult time.

When I was in Talca, Chile, one of the members of a Christian community lost his job. Jobs were almost impossible to find, and this man had a family of six children. The community responded to the family needs, lifted the man out of deep despair, and helped him set up a small home printing business. This man has grown in faith and is now a permanent deacon serving that same community.

Spreading the Good News

Neighborhood Renewal Groups help their members to be apostolic Christians; they want to share their new sense of joy and unity with others. One way is by encouraging other neighbors to experience the Parish Neighborhood Renewal Ministry. Neighborhood Church Community members may volunteer to join the mission team, and they also may help finance the expenses of the Renewal Core Team.

Outreach to Youth

Young people are often, paradoxically, the neighborhood's greatest pride and biggest headache. To leave them alone is not wise.

Adults must get involved with them: Young people need good models to imitate. Some members of the Neighborhood Church Community should be given specific responsibility for the various aspects of youth involvement. Some of these aspects are religious education; youth group activity such as scouting, social recreation, and youth-center supervision; and coaching sports. Some Neighborhood Church Communities have looked into the content of school courses—especially the moral teachings—in order to take appropriate action.

One Neighborhood Church Community examined the approaches of other Christian denominations to see why some programs were attracting the youth. With this information they hoped to revitalize their own Catholic youth program.

Young people usually compare their family rules with rules of nearby families. Then, to back up their pleas for "independence" and greater personal freedom, the youngsters pick and choose from the most liberal guidelines. Through the Neighborhood Church Community, parents can come to agreement on youth conduct and moral limits. This way, parents have a support system for their authority, and teenagers know what is expected of them. Both groups gain by this unified approach to rule making.

Youth Outreach to Youth

The ideal ministry to youth is by youth itself. After a renewal experience, teenagers find it easier to talk with one another about God. Moreover, teenagers often receive the courage to discuss openly the working of God in their lives. To assure that teenage participation continues in a Neighborhood Church Community, the Renewal Core Team recommends that adults try to appreciate the youngsters' time commitments and interests. The Renewal Core Team always includes teenagers in the neighborhood missions; the Neighborhood Church Community should continue this practice.

Brainstorming for Neighborhood Renewal Group Activities

Often the Renewal Core Team finds that new communities have a limited vision of their potential in working for Jesus Christ. Here are some possible projects to help beginners brainstorm their own activities.

1. Social sharing in get-togethers, picnics, entertainments, Christmas caroling.
2. Traffic-speed reduction by placing signs, traffic lights, and road bumps for slowing and controlling the speeding.
3. Vigilance and crime reduction.
4. Control of drug traffic and alcoholic beverages for minors.
5. Protection of the neighborhood from hazardous wastes and other health, environmental, and safety hazards.
6. Better transportation for the neighborhood.
7. Elimination of racial discrimination in housing and institutions.
8. Elimination of pornography.
9. Obtaining and upkeep of recreational facilities.
10. Building up of the neighborhood's pride
    a. Maintenance of a clean neighborhood.
    b. Beautification of apartments and houses with outdoor landscaping.
11. Formation of a neighborhood cooperative for bettering local life by providing:
    a. Food products.
    b. Chemicals to save trees; for example, in Dutch elm disease prevention.
    c. Garden-club materials.
12. Outreach beyond the neighborhood
    a. Reaching out to help another area in the town or inner city.
    b. Sponsoring of a refugee family.
    c. Participating in Pro-Life activities.
13. Performance of the corporal works of mercy
    a. Visit the sick and dying.
    b. Visit the prisoners.

  c. Clothe the naked.
  d. Feed the hungry.
  e. Bury the dead.
14. Establishment of an information resource center for poverty
    cases.
15. Study and cultural activities
  a. Coming together for continuing education: Scripture shar-
     ing, hobbies, sharing of interests.
  b. Reaching out to others: teaching CCD; preparing people
     for marriage, faith instructions, teaching the handicapped.
16. Involvement in the ministry, which calls for
  a. Hospitality; incorporation of new arrivals in the
     neighborhood.
  b. Holy Communion ministers to go to the sick and aged.
  c. Evangelization team members for visiting and helping to
     give Parish Neighborhood Renewal missions and other
     parish evangelization programs.
  d. Consolation for those suffering from deaths and
     separations.
  e. Group participation in parish activities. (One group
     accepted responsibility of the liturgical decoration of the
     church for the principal seasons and thus freed the parish
     staff from this work. Others could care for various parish
     needs by group projects such as festivals, financing, and
     building maintenance.)
  f. All types of counseling: youth, single-parent homes, birth-
     right, chemical dependency, and retirement adjustment.
17. Spiritual sharing
  a. Sharing of love with the unloved and with one another.
  b. Praying together with next-door neighbors.
  c. Sharing the joys and needs of one another in God.
  d. Forming prayer teams for the healing ministry.
  We have been called to become prophets in our own time. St.
Paul defines the prophet as one who builds up, encourages, and
consoles. As Jesus says, "You are the light of the world. Your light
must shine before men so that they may see goodness in your
acts and give praise to your heavenly Father" (Matthew 5:14,
16).

CHAPTER TEN

Joyful Christians Bring New Life to the Parish

I kneel before the Father from whom every family in heaven and on earth takes its name; and I pray that he will bestow on you gifts in keeping with the riches of his glory. May he strengthen you inwardly through the working of his Spirit. May Christ dwell in your hearts through faith, and may charity be the root and foundation of your life. Thus you will be able to grasp fully, with all the holy ones, the breadth and length and height and depth of Christ's love, and experience this love which surpasses all knowledge, so that you may attain to the fullness of God himself.

—Ephesians 3:14-19

When parishioners, pastors, parish staffs, and renewal teams all pray for the outpouring of the Holy Spirit on their parishes, God's power becomes real to them. In this chapter I would like to share some of the experiences and changes that take place among pastors and pastoral staffs, among the laity, among families, in the neighborhoods, and in the parishes that have experienced our renewal program.

Impact on Pastors and Pastoral Staffs

One pastor describes the results of the Parish Neighborhood Renewal Ministry as follows:

Church time is more joyful; people are listening more. At the greeting of peace, there is more warmth. As the Neighborhood Church Communities continue meeting, people are more comfortable with one another and seem to care more for one another. I see the "Good News" spreading.

Father John Dolsina comments that he has seen a new attitude at Mass, especially at daily Mass. "I see more participation, more interest, and greater numbers." Daily Mass attendance has doubled in his parish, and he attributes this increase to the Parish Neighborhood Renewal Ministry.

Another diocesan priest says:

There is excitement in my parish. The support that the Neighborhood Renewal Ministry offers is good for us. There is a real affirmation of faith. Individuals in the Neighborhood Church Communities receive growth from one another. It satisfies the desire people have for a deeper relationship with God.

Pastors find a new and valuable form of leadership springing up in servant-leaders. The servant-leader is usually a very likeable person, more person-oriented than task-oriented. Moreover, he or she is well accepted by the neighborhood. The pastor sees these responsible people taking on ministries and serving Neighborhood Church; they serve willingly and give a new boost to parish spirit. Their meetings are different from the usual lay meetings because renewal rather than business details is emphasized.

Because the pastor and staff have participated in the prayer and mission process, they themselves have experienced deep changes. Their interpersonal relationships are more understanding and loving. Awe and wonder at the Holy Spirit's work in their parish leads them to a new vision of parish life. Often a deeper appreciation for and intensity of prayer emerges from the Parish Neighborhood Renewal program. Usually staff members experience healing through group prayer and as a result exhibit increased freedom and joy in their work; the parishioners notice this change of attitude.

Two Franciscan sisters who work with Neighborhood Church Communities experienced personal changes. Sister Fran Sulzer relates, "My faith has been intensified as I have become more conscious of the action of the Holy Spirit in my life." Her companion, Sister Joan Weisenbeck, says, "The Spirit of the early Christian communities is at work in our parish here, and I am challenged to continue growing with my people."

The Laity Are Changed

Parishioners experience change in the core of their being. As one priest puts it, "My people have more happiness, peace, faith openness, and they pray spontaneously."

The lay person has a feeling of closeness to Jesus; religion becomes a way of life and not a series of isolated acts. Enthusiasm for the opportunity of meeting with neighbors and joy in serving them are evident. Mass and sacraments take on new significance. In short, the individual finds a new way of life.

Another change for the lay person is the sense of participating in the parish as a member of the faith community. Loneliness leaves the renewed lay person as he or she senses God's presence in the Neighborhood Church Community. One of Father John Dolsina's parishioners stated, "We have been meeting weekly for about a year now, and the Community has really become a part of our life. In fact, to miss our neighborhood meeting would leave a great void in our lives."

The Family Is Pulled Together

Perhaps one of the most significant factors in the success of the Neighborhood Church Community is that the family, often divided by activities, is brought together with other neighborhood families. We have frequently seen the entire range of ages, from small children to the elderly, all enjoying their time together. The individual family itself is also more united by spending time together, especially time in prayer. A sense of responsibility is often instilled in the whole family. They are Church, and Jesus is present. For example, one family was suffering because a son was chemically dependent. Each member was praying individually for the son, yet there was no progress. After a Parish Neighborhood Renewal mission the family of seven decided to pray together daily for this young teenager. Within two weeks he agreed to get help and began treatment. The family members truly felt the power of praying together in Jesus' name. The family also appreciated the support of the Neighborhood Church Community that joined with them in prayer.

Mrs. Dorothy Kopp decribes the enjoyment felt by her two gradeschoolers and one teenage son when they attend the weekly neighborhood meetings.

My children look forward to being treated as equal members of the group. The meetings are fun, and we introduce games, with the prize being the right to choose a scripture passage and then read it for reflection of the group. The youth members also have the opportunity of choosing songs, and they sing them with gusto!

The Neighborhood Begins to Change

A sense of friendliness first permeates the Neighborhood Church Community and then radiates into the whole neighborhood. People begin to reach out to their neighbors.

The outreach of the Neighborhood Church Community has a spiritual dimension and a social thrust. Many prayers are answered. Light dispels darkness, and certainly each group is a source of light to the neighborhood. (For example, in one city a newly formed group in a high-crime area saw crime diminish in their housing project. Meanwhile, statistics showed a city-wide increase in crime.) In general, then, the neighborhood takes on a sense of responsibility for all its members—a factor that favors rapid improvement. It is the "domino effect" of lives touching lives.

Neighborhood Renewal Enriches the Parish

As pastor, parish staff, families, and neighborhoods begin to change, so does the parish. Like a transfusion, the blood of new leadership begins to flow through the parish's heart and refreshes its spiritual life. Old routines are renewed, and a new spiritual drive is unleashed. The renewed parishioners want to know Jesus better, to talk about him, to serve him.

New welcome signs are on the doors of the parishioners' hearts. Jesus is not left at the doorstep but is invited to enter. And it is a joyful and permanent visit among these renewed Christians.

THE FUTURE

CHAPTER ELEVEN

The Core Team's Ongoing Contact with the Parish

> I give thanks to my God every time I think of you—which is constantly, in every prayer I utter—rejoicing, as I plead on your behalf, at the way you have all continually helped promote the gospel from the very first day.
>
> —Philippians 1:3-5

St. Paul, as a good evangelizer, continued to nourish the growth of the newly founded Christian communities. In his letters he encouraged the neophytes, he taught them, he urged them to maintain their fidelity to Jesus Christ, and he corrected them when necessary. He prayed for them as well, and visited them when he could.

The Parish Neighborhood Renewal Ministry Core Team feels that same responsibility to those parishes where we have worked. When the initial contract to serve a parish is agreed upon, the Parish Neighborhood Renewal Ministry promises to maintain contact with the parish after the first evangelization period. The Renewal Core Team accomplishes this through days of recollection and workshops. We also agree to return to the parish approximately a year later to work with the servant-leaders for a deepening of their spiritual lives.

The Renewal Core Team focuses on the servant-leaders because they are the dynamic force that keeps parish renewal working. Eager to serve, servant-leaders are often filled with a new vision of Church, so they need solid direction for growth in spirituality. The Renewal Core Team builds, of course, on the pastor's efforts, since he has continued to work with the servant-leaders.

The pastor has been encouraging these servant-leaders through their monthly meetings. In addition, he is responsible for their ongoing education, which he handles personally or delegates to resource persons such as the Renewal Core Team. Pastors should be aware that servant-leaders will feel a need for education in methods of scriptural prayer, dynamics of leadership, and techniques of group spiritual direction. These topics can be treated at the monthly meeting or in a day of recollection. Typically, the pastor involved in renewal work finds an eager reception among the servant-leaders for the Good News he has been preaching to parishioners all along. Priests will find this one of the ironies of renewal!

Three-Part Program for Servant Leaders

The Renewal Core Team always marvels at how God leads the servant-leaders to growth during the first year of Neighborhood Renewal. Nevertheless, many servant-leaders have suffered some deep hurts from criticism or rejection during this period because of their involvement in the renewal. We have seen a husband-wife team of servant-leaders abandoned by their family and friends because they found joy in Jesus and in his message. These hurts are obstacles to the servant-leaders' continued spiritual growth. Thus the healing of these memories and hurts becomes important for continued advancement in the journey with God.

The returning Renewal Core Team presents a three-part program to answer the special needs of the servant-leaders and of the Neighborhood Church Community. First, we offer each servant-leader, together with his or her spouse, the opportunity for the healing of these hurts through prayer for "inner healing." (In the next section I will explain "inner healing" and the process we use.) The second part of our program is a guided retreat for the servant-leaders. We prepare the retreat with a stimulating group of teachings on a spiritual theme, and we provide individual spiritual direction to these leaders. Finally, during our three-week return period the Renewal Core Team visits each Neighborhood Church Community.

The Inner Healing Process

Jesus practiced "inner healing" with the apostles. The classic example is Jesus' appearance to the apostles at the Sea of Tiberias after his resurrection. He asked Simon Peter three times, "Simon, son of John, do you love me more than these?" and after each affirmation by Peter, he showed his confidence in Peter by instructing him, "Feed my lambs" (John 21:15-17).

What was this all about, and what did it heal? The reader has only to recall the events on the night Jesus was seized by the temple guards and led away to be condemned to death. That night Peter denied three times that he was a disciple of Jesus. The triple questioning at the Sea of Tiberias was the process by which Jesus led Peter to wholeness through inner healing.

"Inner healing" or "healing of memories" releases burdened persons from their hurts, memories, and broken relationships. (The Renewal Core Team has found, incidentally, that *every* person needs some sort of inner healing.) Inner healing is considerate and respectful of the person involved. We invite the burdened person to walk with Jesus and allow Jesus to heal the pain. We pray that Jesus will also heal the relationship that was broken with the hurt. The process does not wipe out the memory; rather, it puts the memory in relationship to Jesus so that the incident can be recalled without hurt or anger.

Since peace is also a goal, the Renewal Core Team prefers to place the hurting servant-leaders in surroundings that are pleasant both physically and psychologically. As the individual relaxes, the Renewal Core Team explains the process of inner healing. Next we give the servant-leader ample time to examine himself or herself and to share with the Renewal Core Team any memories that are still sources of hurt and pain. Memory recall in any order is encouraged, because the trained Renewal Core Team will be carefully leading the person backward and forward in time, regardless of the actual chronological sequence of events. The servant-leader is encouraged to share only the principal hurts. This is because inner healing is never finished: New hurts will constantly come to mind. These new hurts can be taken care of in subsequent prayer.

When we judge that sufficient recall has occurred, we help the person to forgive those who have caused the hurt. Unless the person asking for healing is willing to forgive, there can of course be no subsequent healing.

The actual prayer for the healing of hurts and memories is a gentle experience. The hurting servant-leader is led back in imagination, accompanied by Jesus, to the moment and circumstances of each major hurt. This process has been thoroughly explained previously by reminding the servant-leader that God is above our "time quadrant." God is the Beginning and the End of all and is not limited by our human time experience. He reenters at any moment in our lives not only to heal pain but also to repair broken relationships. The Renewal Core Team members try to touch each tender chord in a servant-leader's memory. However, our actions do not limit God's ability to heal. He often brings a fuller healing by treating hurts not even mentioned. We have seen healing prayer transform people's lives from deep hurt and anger to an indwelling of profound peace—with a desire to rebuild broken relationships. Following inner healing, the servant-leader finds himself or herself able to begin this restructuring of relationships and to enter a new level of spiritual growth.

I have found that if a hurt has been caused by a woman, it helps to invite Jesus' mother, Mary, to be present at the reliving of the painful incident. Mary then can pour out the love that was denied by a female relationship. In the same vein, the Renewal Core Team prefers to work in inner healing as a man-woman team. The female team member ministers to those hurts caused by a woman, while the male team member attends to the hurts caused by a man. Male-female teams bring balance to the healing ministry.

We conclude the healing time with a prayer of thanksgiving for the love that God has bestowed. Often inner-healing prayer is a time of deep peace with the Lord. We encourage the servant-leader to spend some quiet time with Jesus in thanksgiving.

When we conduct inner-healing prayer, we need a minimum of one hour for an individual (using the above process) so that a sense of haste will not disrupt the peaceful atmosphere. We usually allow an hour and one-half for a couple. Because our deepest hurts are the ones caused by those closest to us, special emphasis is placed on hurts caused by each spouse when we lead couples through healing prayer.

Group Prayer Brings Inner Healing

A mutual healing occurs when people come together as a group in prayer and sharing. One couple told me:

> We have seen many miracles of inner healing in our neigh-borhood community. Each of us has experienced inner healing in some area of our lives. This did not happen overnight, but as a gradual process in the well-planned time of the Lord. We have come to understand that in group prayer there is a power of praise and petition that surpasses the power of the sum of individual prayers.

When the servant-leaders are freed from their hurts and pains, they feel the presence of Jesus that empowers them to lead their group to a deeper encounter with the Lord. When a servant-leader undergoes inner healing combined with a guided retreat, he or she arrives at a new plane in the spiritual life. Finally, the Neighborhood Church Community as an entity will benefit from the deeper presence of God within its servant-leaders.

The Guided Retreat

The guided retreat combines the advantages of personal direction with group teaching. During the first week in the parish, the returning Renewal Core Team determines the main spiritual needs of the servant-leaders and prepares the guided retreat so as to address those needs.

Besides the group teaching, individual times are allotted to each retreatant for individual direction. The Renewal Core Team gives special importance to this time. Each servant-leader is accepted at his or her present spiritual level and then helped to move into a deeper relationship with God.

Since all activity of the Parish Neighborhood Renewal Ministry takes into consideration the realistic demands of family living, the retreat is designed to keep most mealtimes free. The schedule generally takes up Friday evening, Saturday afternoon and evening, and Sunday afternoon. The meal on Saturday can be potluck or "brown-bagged."

Observations

The servant-leaders are not the only ones to feel criticism and opposition to the renewal efforts. The Renewal Core Team finds that the pastor and staff need affirmation and support in their apostolate, too. Thus times for daily prayer and sharing are set aside for these parish leaders. Often the return of the Renewal Core Team reenergizes staff and lay members of the parish renewal team. During the first year of this renewal program, the parish staff may have found special problems or may need more information. When our Renewal Core Team returns, we supply resource information and materials.

As we contemplate the role of evangelizers, we find that maintaining contact with the parishes served is very important. During the first six-week renewal time in a parish, the Renewal Core Team generates much activity and shares a large quantity of information. Time is needed to assimilate this material in a parish

renewal plan. The continued contact with the Renewal Core
Team helps to clarify the renewal work. The three-week return
period deepens maturity and spirituality in the servant-leaders
and consequently in the whole parish.

A BLESSING FOR MY READERS

I invite you who have read this book to join us as evangelizers—opening doors for Jesus and giving him a joyful welcome. I hope that the Holy Spirit has touched you through this book. May God's love guide you in church renewal! There is only one way that counts, and that is God's way. He is using many different means to call forth his modern-day fishers. The Parish Renewal Ministry is just one of many forms of evangelization called for by Vatican II. The Neighborhood Church Community is a visible work of the Holy Spirit in the Church of today. May the Blessed Virgin Mary accompany and guide you to her son Jesus.

Father Tom Maney, MM

APPENDIX A

The Spirit of the Evangelization Community

We will help the parish establish a model, more or less similar to ours, in which their apostolate flows from a deep prayer life and mutual Christian concern.
> —The Parish Neighborhood Renewal Ministry's
> Statement of Lifestyle, Section 1

In this section I want to draw a clear picture of our Core Team's way of life as an evangelization community.

First, I would like to introduce the original members of our community. How our Renewal Core Team came together is a mystery even we can't explain. After Sister Joan Gerads, OSF, and I began to work in the Duluth, Minnesota, diocese, other evangelizers were attracted to us. Sister Joan and I asked Father Jim Scheuer to be a team member long before we had drawn up the Lifestyle Agreement of our Evangelization Community, but it was a full year later before he received permission from Bishop Paul Anderson to join us. Sister Patricia Schneider, SSND, spent one week with us to see how Neighborhood Renewal worked. She joined us in September of 1979. Mrs. Anna Chernugal attended our first workshop on Neighborhood Renewal in Little Falls, Minnesota. Despite severe thunderstorms, she finally drove in from Hibbing, Minnesota, hours late but determined to join us. Anna became our first lay Renewal Core Team member. Eugene Skelton of St. Cloud, Minnesota, as chairman of the

Evangelization Committee of St. Augustine's Parish, invited us to work in his parish and ended up joining our Renewal Core Team.

We six original members have developed a simple, prayerful, and sharing lifestyle. We have chosen to share life in an evangelization community. As members of that community, each of us is called to foster the growth and happiness of the others. Since we believe that we are our "brother's keeper," we also believe we must first show genuine love within our community. Certainly we must live in a loving community before we can expect others to follow our example. In our community life, both asking forgiveness and granting pardon are essential daily acts. Ideally, each evening we gather together to ask God to heal the hurts we have suffered in the apostolate; we pray that he will sustain us in the coming day.

Perhaps I can best catch the spirit of the Renewal Core Team's choice of values and lifestyle in these words of St. Paul to Timothy:

> There is, of course, great gain in religion—provided one is content with a sufficiency. We brought nothing into this world, nor have we the power to take anything out. If we have food and clothing we have all that we need. The love of money is the root of all evil. . . . Flee from all this. Instead, seek after integrity, piety, faith, love, steadfastness, and a gentle spirit. Fight the good fight of faith. Take firm hold on the everlasting life to which you were called when, in the presence of many witnesses, you made your noble profession of faith.
>
> —1 Timothy 6:6-8, 10-12

Now a more detailed description of both our values and our lifestyle may enable the reader better to understand our total philosophy.

The Core Team's Spiritual Values

1. We experience God as a personal God who is vitally interested

in what we are doing. He has called us into this renewal work at this time in history as part of his divine plan. He will support this work as long as he wishes it to continue. God wants his people to come together in his name much more than they do.

2. Our prayer responds to God's love. God, in turn, hears our prayers and acts on them. The parish team quickly sees that the miracles of the New Testament are still occurring today for those who have faith in God. This faith, evidenced in prayer, is a communal act as well as a private experience, so we set aside time for both group and individual prayer.

3. Those who try to help people to move into a deeper union with God will be criticized, ridiculed, and attacked. Our Renewal Core Team and our associates in this renewal work are in a true spiritual warfare, but we who love God do not fear opposition: Jesus has given us power in his name. Nevertheless, in renewal work we evangelizers will often feel oppressed. For this reason we pray daily for one another's well-being and for the strength of perseverance. We believe in the power of intercessory prayer and the need for redemptive suffering. Shared prayer-power is one advantage of working with an evangelization community.

4. We teach the parish team to be aware that the servant-leaders need spiritual direction and healing prayer. Pastoral support in these spiritual dimensions must be given if the servant-leaders are to experience continued growth. We assume that the renewed priest or parish team member has attended spiritual-direction courses or workshops and therefore understands the importance of this growth-giving ministry.

5. Our Renewal Core Team always asks the bishop's permission to work in his diocese. From the very beginning we want his suggestions and blessing upon this work; then we keep him informed of our actions. We offer special prayer for the bishop because Jesus entrusted to his authority the unity of the diocesan family, neighborhood, and parish Churches. We further recognize the authority of the pastor as a visible sign of unity for the Neighborhood Church. Our Renewal Core Team is an instrument for strengthening church unity by *always* working under proper church authority.

6. "All Christians, by the very nature of their vocations, are called to the apostolate. The laity must not only be allowed to practice their vocation but if they do not, they are neither useful to the Church nor themselves" (*Documents of Vatican II*, "Decree on the Apostolate of the Laity," paragraph 2). We encourage each person—single or married—to reach out to others, to become part of the parish renewal team, and to continue the renewal efforts after the Renewal Core Team departs. The world will be renewed in Jesus Christ only when the laity brings the spirit of renewal into the factories, businesses, labor unions, neighborhoods, schools, hospitals, farms, apartment buildings, and houses where people live and work.

The Parish Neighborhood Renewal Core Team's Statement of Lifestyle

I. Introductory Statement

The core group comes together to bear witness to and to grow in the Lord as an evangelization community. We believe that our life itself must *be* a Christian community if we are to be effective witnesses and teachers of Christian living. Therefore we usually minister as teams. Our apostolate is based on prayer and flows forth from it, principally in assisting in the establishment of Neighborhood Church Communities. Ordinarily this is done in two stages: (1) a six-week initial period for beginning a limited number of neighborhood communities, followed by a six-month consultation service; (2) a three-week period for the formation of servant-leaders, about six months after the initial period.

Our aim is to leave in each parish a committed team which will continue parish neighborhood renewal in union with and in support of the pastor. We will help establish a model (more or less similar to ours) in which the apostolate flows from deep prayer and mutual Christian concern.

The following model expresses our lifestyle that we share with communities as we are called out to serve them. Once every three months the core group comes together for an entire week to live this lifestyle intensely; during the rest of the time our lifestyle will be adapted according to local circumstances in our work in the parishes.

II. The Apostolate of the Core Group
Our apostolate will include:
A. Parish renewal through establishment of Neighborhood Church Communities open to the Spirit.
B. Establishment of structures for growth of servant-leaders and continued evangelization, including ongoing contact with Neighborhood Church Communities we have established.
C. Widening of the aspect of service in the communities through a personal prayer ministry accompanied by healing workshops and encouragement for people to enter aspects of prayer ministry.
D. Continuation of the deepening of Christian commitment for those who have made a neighborhood retreat. To this end, we encourage assistance at Cursillos, Life in the Spirit Seminars, Marriage Encounters, scripture studies, social outreach missions, etc.
E. The sharing with priests, bishops, and others of information and help for renewal wherever readiness and the Spirit lead.
F. The reaching out in ecumenical effort as the Spirit leads us, in accord with the Vatican II documents.
G. The giving of spiritual direction, retreats, conferences, and workshops as time allows and as mutual discernment indicates.
H. Contribution to the renewal of our own religious order and/ or diocesan community.

III. Style of Life of the Core Group
A. Prayer
Our prayer will include:
1. Shared prayer based on an orderly reading of Scripture and spontaneous prayer for one hour (or more) daily.

2. Eucharist together daily.

3. Private prayer for time desired.

4. Office (Liturgy of the Hours) together daily.

5. Fasting.

6. Sunrise and outdoor prayer as inspired.

7. Prayer for one another's needs.

B. Recreation

Our recreation will include:

1. Recreation of spirit, mind, and body.

2. Some time daily for physical recreation and mental relaxation.

3. One day during the week together for fun.

4. Other recreation as the Spirit and our companionship lead.

C. Education

Our education will include:

1. Study and reflection together on *Documents of Vatican II* and related documents.

2. Study and sharing of the Scriptures.

3. Study of the history and culture of the people among whom we live and work.

4. Continued preparation in individual areas of need (in theology, personal interest, and professional growth).

5. Attendance at such diocesan, regional, national, and international assemblies as are open to the Spirit, so that contact is maintained with the Spirit in the Church.

D. Service

Our service will include:

1. Service of one another to foster the growth and happiness of all. We will make an annual commitment.

2. Incorporation of the prayer of abandonment of Charles de Foucould and the Prayer of St. Francis.

3. Daily prayer for the healing of one another and for the support of the apostolic endeavors of one another.

4. A consecration to the Blessed Virgin Mary.

E. Simplicity of Life

Our simplicity of life mandates that:

1. We will not own a physical center or house but rather will accept what is provided.
2. As we move around we will try to use public modes of transportation unless the use of private car, etc., would enhance the apostolate.
3. We will each aim to grow in simplicity of life as the Spirit directs us, without either imposing our own way of life on others or hampering individual leadings.
4. As we move about, we will accept what is provided in food, lodging, etc., trusting that the Lord will help us obtain what we need for our lives and ministry if it is not readily offered.
5. Each member of the core team will be conscious of the need to obtain additional funds to meet the commitments of the ministry.

F. Order and Schedule of the Community Week Held Every Three Months

1. One day in poustinia. ("Poustinia" refers to a separate room or small structure, very basic in furnishings and somewhat isolated in location, set apart for an individual who wishes long periods of private prayer.)
2. One day of recreation.
3. Five days of scheduled Liturgy of the Hours and Eucharist.
4. Five days of scheduled prayer in the morning.
5. During these five days, scheduled time will include:
    study
    cultural activity
    review of life
    planning
    time with the bishop
    reports and faith sharing
6. During the three-month period, each member is encouraged to take one additional week of free time, prayer, and recreation at his or her convenience.
7. Every three months, we rotate the leadership needed to coordinate activities during the ensuing three months and to organize the culminating week of retreat.

IV. Financing

Preamble: We believe that the decision to accept a work is to be based on discernment of God's will and not on ability to pay a fee. Stipends received from parishes are negotiated.

We have budgeted a monthly stipend to be given to our religious orders. This is a suggested sum that can be negotiated according to amounts received from the parishes. Money needed for personal expenses will be received from our religious orders.

A monthly stipend will be negotiated with the lay members to help them meet living expenses.

APPENDIX B

Mission of Renewal in the Holy Spirit to Initiate Basic Church Communities

This mission was planned to be given within a neighborhood, taking into account the concerns of the participants regarding time required, physical distances to be traveled, etc. The following are some important considerations for the mission team.

1. The Duration: The mission is given for one and one-half hours each night for five nights. It should be scheduled to begin at the time most convenient for the participants.

2. The Place: The participants should choose the place most convenient for themselves, even though it may be inconvenient for the team. The place can be a private home, a school, or even an outdoor site.

3. The Nightly Meeting: Of the hour and one-half meeting, forty-five minutes are allotted for the presentations and forty-five minutes for prayer in which the participants are assisted to pray out loud. Each meeting includes lively songs, prayers of thanksgiving, prayers of petition, and the parish prayer of renewal. These are interspersed between the presentations. The placement and amount of time given to these activities varies as the community forms. Everything is done in a spirit of prayer, with the participants made conscious of the Holy Spirit working in the heart of each person present. A powerful way to begin each presentation is with a reading from the Scriptures followed by reflection, since the Word of God is more important than the word of any other person. The team

aims to present Jesus to the group and then allow him to touch their hearts.

4. The Team: The team is composed of priests, religious, and lay persons (adults and teenagers). The team meets each night before the scheduled mission meeting to pray for the team and for the participants.

   a. The themes of the evening are distributed among the members of the team (usually on the previous evening).

   b. The team prays for the liberation of the people of the neighborhood, for the team, and for the power and the gifts of the Holy Spirit. The team needs these special gifts for preaching, for discerning the needs of the group, and for healing. Thus the teachings of God's goodness will be confirmed.

   c. The team members expect that the Spirit will guide them, changing and modifying the themes, e.g., to interior healing, liberation, changes in the Church, etc.

5. The Parish Priest: It is important to do everything in cooperation with the parish priest. Life and growth in the Spirit greatly depend on him. If he is so disposed, he is incorporated into the team.

6. Follow-up after the Termination of the Mission: The purpose of the mission is to sow a seed of Christian community in the heart of the neighborhood. Its growth depends on the Holy Spirit and on the support of the parish priest and other parish members.

   Experience has taught us that it is best to have responsible persons from the neighborhood itself lead the regular meetings after the termination of the mission. They need the support of and contact with the pastor. It is suggested that the pastor begin regular monthly meetings with the servant-leaders of all the neighborhood groups to allow them to exchange experiences, to pray together, to learn, and to open themselves more to the gifts and ministries of the Spirit.

First Night:
Jesus the Answer for a Troubled World

Presentations:

1. The results of sin around us in the world, city, and neighborhood. Lack of unity and trust among people in a mobile
society. The presence of hope in the message of renewal and
Vatican II (1 Peter 2:9-10; James 4:1-3). Our call to be a sign of
Christlike strength in the midst of such a world. How can we
better answer that call?
2. God's love for us. Jesus' being sent as the answer to the
problems of the world (John 3:16-17 and 14:6). Jesus present in
the neighborhood and in us (Matthew 18:19-20).
3. Jesus' teaching us to ask that our joy may be full; to pray and to
relate to God as Father; to beseech God for forgiveness, with
persistence (Luke 11:1-13). God's desire that we ask for help in
our needs (John 14:13-14; 15:7-8; 16:23-24).

Group Activity:
Invitation to all to join in prayer, both spontaneous and guided.
Prayer of the community for the sick who are present.

Second Night:
Jesus (Healer) Yesterday and Today

Presentations:
1. Jesus' sending His Spirit to live within us (1 John 3:24). God's
intention that our bodies be fitting temples of the Holy Spirit (1
Corinthians 3:16-17; 6:19-20). The Spirit praying in us, helping
us to pray (Romans 8:27-28).
2. The compassion of Jesus for the sick. Jesus' never sending
anyone away who asked for healing and help: the deaf-mute
(Mark 7:31-37); the blind man (Mark 8:22-26).
3. Sharings from any of the sick who were healed or improved.
4. The call to pray for the sick (James 5:13-16). Manner in which
parents can pray for sick children in the family, and neighbors
for one another.

Group Activity:
Participation in spontaneous prayer and community prayer for
the sick present and for the neighborhood.

Third Night:
An Encounter with Jesus and Its Effect

Presentations:
1. Sharing of new life in the Holy Spirit (by mission team members).
2. Jesus and the Samaritan woman (John 4:7-30, 39-42). An ordinary woman offered new life by Jesus. Her mode of response.
3. Nicodemus and Jesus (John 3:1-8). A respectable man with solid social status, ashamed to be found changing. The experience of being born again. The way he changes (John 7:50; 19:39). Optional: Jesus and Zacchaeus (Luke 19:1-10). Important man, hated by his own, taking advantage of his own. Leaves all and is willing to stand up and proclaim his conversion.
4. Today, because of Jesus, the same Holy Spirit changing us. (Select one: Galatians 5:16-26; Ephesians 5:1-20; Ephesians 3:14-21). Gives us peace and joy and a new desire to pray and read Scripture; inspires us to witness to his presence in us; grants us a sense of community, unity with our neighbors.

Group Activity:
Participation in spontaneous, shared prayer.

Fourth Night:
Renewal in the Spirit
(Baptism in the Spirit)

Presentations:
1. Sharings of new life in the Spirit.
2. Pentecost, the coming of the Spirit (Acts 1:3-8, 14; 2:1-18). Mary's presence; the apostles without power to give testimony of God (Peter and Thomas); the Spirit empowering one to witness (Acts 1:8). Baptism and baptism in the Spirit. This new life of the Spirit intended for everyone (Acts 2:39).

3. Explanation of the new life in the Spirit and the action of the Spirit to form community—Body of Christ (Numbers 11:10-17, 24-30).

Group Activity:
1. Prayer of reconciliation (closest person, family, associates and neighbors, people who have hurt us).
2. Renewal of baptismal promises.
3. Prayer for the renewal of the Spirit in our lives and the lives of those in the whole neighborhood.

Fifth Night:
The Neighborhood Church Community

Presentations:
1. Sharings of new life in the Spirit.
2. A Christian community formed and guided by the Spirit (Acts 2:42). Prayer (Colossians 3:16-17; Ephesians 5:19-20). Breaking of the bread; coming together in Eucharist; teaching of the apostles; importance of study and classes; sharing with one another (Acts 2:43-47).
3. The gifts of the Spirit active in the community: wisdom, counsel, healing, prophecy, tongues (1 Corinthians 12:3-11 or Romans 12:3-8). The gifts of the Spirit as aids in serving and living community.

Group Activity:
1. Celebrate Eucharist if appropriate (simple, family style).
2. Choose three responsible men to begin calling the Neighborhood Church Community together.
3. Pray for gifts that the Neighborhood Church Community wishes and needs.

4. Set a place, time, and date for the next Neighborhood Church Community meeting.

Father Ralph Rogawski, OP

Sister Helen Raycraft, OP

Adapted by the Parish Neighborhood Renewal Core Team

APPENDIX C

Flow Chart
and Checklist for Flow Chart

Flow Chart
for the Formation of Neighborhood Church
Communities

(Consult the Checklist on pages 100-101 for *details* of the steps in this Flow Chart.)

I. *Six months* before beginning the Parish Neighborhood Renewal mission:
   1. Have the parish renewal prayer printed (5,000 for a large parish).
   2. Begin prayer preparation: Distribute the parish renewal prayer and saturate the parish with prayer.
   3. Begin the information and attitude-formation campaign.

II. *One month* before beginning the PNR mission: Obtain the necessary materials to begin renewal. (See Checklist).

III. *Two weeks* before the mission:
   1. Hold a general parish meeting:
      a. Explain the process of renewal.
      b. Sign up volunteers: home visitors, host homes, one mission team.

2. Select the first host home. (See Checklist.)
3. Establish the intercessory prayer and teaching group. (Most home visitors will come from this group.)
4. Form the first mission team.

IV. *One week* before the mission:
Visit all the Catholic families and parishioners in the neighborhood. (See Checklist.)

V. *Weekend* before the mission:
Revisit the host home. (See Checklist.)

VI. *Beginning the mission:*
1. *At least one day before the mission:* Meet with the mission team. The team prays for the mission and is assigned presentations.
2. *Each night of the mission:* Meet with the mission team 45 minutes before the session to pray and to plan the flow of the session.
3. The team goes to the mission united in prayer.
4. The team brings materials. (See Checklist.)

VII. *Immediately after each mission session:*
The mission team meets. (See Checklist.)

VIII. *Concluding the mission*—forming Neighborhood Church Community (NCC):
At the end of the final session, hold a brief meeting with the newly chosen servant-leaders of the NCC. (See Checklist.)

IX. *Monthly:*
Servant-leaders meet with the pastor.

X. *Every three months:*
Have a retreat day for servant-leaders and members of the NCCs.

XI. *After six months to a year:*
Conduct a follow-up growth experience for servant-leaders. (See Checklist.)

* * *

Checklist for Flow Chart

(Roman numerals below correspond to those on the Flow Chart on pages 98-99.)

II. Necessary materials for the initial six missions:
1. New Testaments—200.
2. Parish renewal prayer—5,000 for a large parish.
3. Song sheets—1,000.
4. Mission invitation slips—1,000.

III, 2. Selecting the host home:
1. Visit the family; be sure the husband is present.
2. Pray for the home on the first visit to the neighborhood.
3. Explain what is and is not expected of the host home.
4. Obtain a commitment to assist all five sessions of the mission.
5. Decide with the family the neighborhood's boundaries.

IV. Visiting the neighborhood:
1. Prepare maps and visitings lists for the visitors.
2. Hold a meeting for the visitors: Pray, explain how to visit; send out visitors two by two.
3. Upon the return of the teams, have song, prayer, and reports on the visits.
4. When the whole neighborhood has been visited, make three typewritten copies of the list of homes visited: one each for the pastor, host family, and files.

V. Revisiting the host home:
1. Give the host family a list of the homes visited.
2. Leave a mission cross.
3. Review and clarify the host's responsibilities.

4. Have the host family invite neighbors, especially men to men.

VI,4. Materials for the mission:
   1. New Testaments—50.
   2. Parish renewal prayer—50.
   3. Song sheets—50.

VII. Team meeting immediately after each mission session:
   1. Open with a song.
   2. Say a prayer of thanksgiving.
   3. Discern how the Holy Spirit moved in the session.
   4. Ask for suggestions for improving the next session.
   5. Assign presentations for the next session.

VIII. Meeting with the newly chosen servant-leaders of the NCC at the end of the final session:
   1. Decide the day, hour, and place of the next *weekly* meeting.
   2. Review the basic elements of the *one-hour* NCC meeting.
   3. Leave enough song sheets, renewal prayers, and New Testaments for the future neighborhood meetings.

XI. Follow-up growth experience for servant-leaders after six months to a year:
   1. Conduct inner healing prayer sessions.
   2. Conduct a retreat that leads the NCC to an outreach commitment.
   3. Pastor attends one meeting of each NCC.